Declutter Your Way To Success

The Keys to Organize Your Life

Scripture quotations, unless otherwise noted are taken from THE HOLY BIBLE, NEW INTERNATIONAL VERSION®, NIV® Copyright © 1973, 1978, 1984, 2011 by Biblica, Inc.® Used by permission. All rights reserved worldwide.

Original ISBN 13: 978-1-942126-10-2
ISBN 13 International Tradepaper Edition: 978-1-6803-1469-4

Terri Savelle Foy Ministries
Post Office Box 1959
Rockwall, TX 75087
www.terri.com

Printed in the United States of America
First Edition 2017

Declutter Your Way To Success

The Keys to Organize Your Life

Introduction

If you want to change the world, start off by making your bed.
Admiral Bill McRaven (Navy SEAL)

It's intriguing to me that the first directive I ever heard from the Lord as I began my journey in personal growth was *not* about making a major impact in the nation of France, translating our books to French, speaking in French churches all the way from the French Riviera to the streets of downtown Paris, or providing French subtitles to our weekly podcast.

The clear instruction that brought significant promotion to my life was *not* to launch a worldwide television broadcast that would air in over 200 nations or for my shy self to start getting comfortable communicating in front of a camera.

The pivotal command was *not* to get my hands on as many leadership books as possible because one day I would employ teams of people. Nor was it to immerse myself in knowledge about how to design a vision board because one day I would take that teaching around the world.

None of that was brought to my attention (or even a part of my future dreams and goals) at the time. However, I did receive one unsubtle, clear-cut, vivid statement that would prove to be the prerequisite for my success:

Declutter Your Way To Success

Clean up and clean out.

Yes, that was my first God-given vision for my life on earth. To clean! I know, I wasn't thrilled about it either. In fact, I even questioned, "Is that truly the voice of God or the voice of my mom?" But seriously, I was unsure if I could truly hear God's voice and if I could, is that really what He would instruct me to do with my life? Disinfect. Scrub. Fold. Scour.

At a time when my life was falling apart, my marriage was on the verge of divorce and I had no particular goals to pursue, those five words became my vision, my aim, my daily motivation. Since that day, I have discovered that there is a direct link between organization and success.

I have read numerous success books which clearly advise, recommend, and demand that cleaning up the clutter in your life and becoming a person of excellence is a requirement for promotion.

So, I want to help you defeat the overwhelm of clutter, put an end to procrastination, and make excellence a standard in your everyday life. Why? So that you're in shape, prepared, and ready to seize your much-anticipated, earned and deserved promotion!

Chapter 1

Proven for Promotion

Before anything else, preparation is the key to success.
Alexander Graham Bell

Before our military trains their soldiers to fight in mortal combat, they must first go through extensive training in "Bed Making 101." Nobody makes a bed neater than our armed forces. Basic training doesn't only have to do with drills and weapons, but also making a bed with proper "forty-five-degree hospital corners." Why is that? What is the big deal? Is the enemy going to be impressed by the old "bounce a quarter off the bed" trick? It is because it instills a standard of excellence.

The bottom line: The way you do *anything* is the way you do everything.

Imagine walking into the barracks of the United States Army and seeing mattresses with unmade beds, sheets in a pile, wadded up blankets, and last night's clothes thrown on the floor (similar to that of a typical teenage boy). What kind of impression would that give you of the safety of our country? Are we in the hands of the elite or the hands of defeat?

If you're sloppy about making your bed, you'll be sloppy

about loading your rifle. A cluttered environment is the sign of a cluttered mind. That's why they give strict attention to details in every area of training. Army Sergeant Shane Medders said, "Making a military rack (aka bed) is used mainly for uniformity purposes. To make sure that everyone is in-line together, all the same, and for purposes of cleanliness."[1]

Admiral Bill McRaven is the former head of the Joint U.S. Special Operations Command, a 36-year SEAL who commanded a squadron in the fabled Naval Special Warfare Development Group, better known as SEAL Team Six, as well as overseeing the plan and execution of the raid that killed Osama bin Laden.

Some say he is also the most "mysterious and guarded" Navy four-star admiral. He tends to shy away from the media which is why it was such a rare treat for the University of Texas at Austin to include him in their commencement speech. As he began teaching 10 lessons he learned during his SEAL training, his speech echoed these profound words from such a tough, intimidating soldier, "If you want to change the world, start off by making your bed."

Admiral McRaven continued, "If you make your bed every morning, you will have accomplished the first task of the day. It will give you a small sense of pride, and it will encourage you to do another task and another and another."[2] It's not just about housekeeping; it's about your personal standard. Your level of respect for yourself and your family shows up in your surroundings.

Keep in mind, we are pursuing excellence, not perfection. Excellence is simply doing ordinary, everyday, mundane tasks in an extraordinary way.

Proven for Promotion

Once you have experienced excellence,
you will never again be content with mediocrity.
Thomas Monson

As I mentioned in the introduction, my first directive in the journey of personal growth was to get cleaned up. That does not sound the least bit exciting or compelling. It sounded futile knowing how far I needed to go in my life. This instruction came at a time when I was blatantly miserable. My marriage was on the verge of divorce. I was confused, hurt, unhappy, and in dire need of vision.

I didn't have a success coach come to my house and lay out a growth track for me to follow. I didn't have a mentor lead me in this strategic plan. I didn't have a simple book telling me that five words could transform my mental health, my energy, my relationships, and even set me on a career path that would boggle my mind! I didn't even have an indication of what God wanted me to do with my life.

All I knew was that I heard those five words, "Clean up and clean out," and that became all the direction I needed for that season of my life.

I took those words literally and seriously. I began with one room, one day, one section at a time. I started with the kitchen. In addition to my cleaning products, my broom, my mop, and my latex gloves, I carried a CD player loaded with faith-building audio messages. I wanted to renew my mind of all the painful thoughts I was entertaining, restore my focus, and rebuild my faith. Since "faith comes by hearing" (Romans 10:17), I couldn't help but get stronger on the inside as I began cleaning on the outside.

With the kitchen being my first vision, I stayed focused on

that room alone. As I would carry items from the kitchen that belonged in other rooms of the house, the tendency would be to start cleaning that other disorganized space, but I had to say, "No, Terri, stay focused on one room alone until it is excellent."

I transferred the stack of bills laying across the kitchen desk to a designated drawer in the office. I hung the car keys on a hook in the laundry room. I took the jogging shoes (laying by the kitchen table) up to the closet where they belonged. I hung the jackets in the coat closet instead of draped over a kitchen chair. I loaded the dishwasher. I cleaned off the countertops. I emptied out the refrigerator of old, outdated food, and leftover take-out boxes from restaurants. I sprayed, scrubbed, wiped down every square inch of the stubborn ketchup spills and strawberry leaks in the bottom of the drawers. I had trash bags full of nearly empty bottles, cartons and FasTaco nachos in Styrofoam containers taking up wasted space in the refrigerator.

When I moved on to the kitchen pantry, I filled another trash bag of stale chips, outdated cereal boxes, old cans of tomato sauce, and bread bags with one moldy bun left at the bottom.

I was on a mission. I was energized by each section of cleanliness. I was disgusted by the disarray. I was motivated by vision. And I was being transformed by the Word of God in the process. Every square inch was clean and in order. The floors were mopped, the appliances were wiped down, the counters were cleared off, the window blinds were opened and a candle was lit. I felt a sense of confidence. I was pleased and proud to visibly see my progress. It brought such peace into my home and into my mind.

Getting my kitchen in order did more for me mentally than it did physically. I felt charged up. Although my circumstances were still a huge mess, I had order in this area of my life and that gave me serenity. Once that tedious but profitable process was complete, it was time to move on to room number two: my bedroom.

I had made a list of each room of the house and what needed to be done in order to make it clean and excellent. There's just something about having it written down and the thrill of making that check mark of completion that stirs me up! I was eager to get up the next day and start conquering the clutter in my bedroom.

Again, I carried my little CD player and pushed play. I started with the clutter I could see. The shoes on the floor, the clothes laying across the chair, the change on top of the dresser, the empty glass on the nightstand, the dried-up candle jars with nothing left to burn. Once the visible clutter was picked up, I could instantly see my progress and that motivated me to keep going.

I attacked the dresser drawers that had become junky and disorganized. I not only folded each piece of clothing, but I began four piles: keep, give, trash or sell. I designated each item for one of the four categories and then loaded them in trash bags. The remaining pieces I kept were folded nicely and stored in the drawers.

In the following chapters, I will walk you through this process of organization, but first I wanted you to see how detailed I was in following through with my directive from God. After every single room, closet, drawer, and cabinet in my entire home was (what I would define as) clean and excellent, I had more peace than ever before. I wouldn't need to apologize to unexpected visitors. I could truly rest without the guilt of needing to get things cleaned. I could start thinking more about my future rather than how much I needed to do at home.

And I had no idea that exactly nine months after that (seemingly petty) instruction, I would be promoted as the CEO of an international ministry overseeing eight offices around the world!

God was truly proving me for promotion. He was observing how I could manage small things in order to lead greater things.

You might be asking, "Terri, you couldn't become a Senior Vice President until you got your sock drawer organized?" Our handbook for life says, "If you are faithful in *little* things, you will be faithful in *large* ones. But if you are dishonest in little things, you won't be honest with greater responsibilities" (Luke 16:10, NLT, emphasis mine). Another translation says, "Whoever can be trusted with very little can also be trusted with much."

If I couldn't get my house in order, how could I get an organization in order? If I was a mess, my leadership would be a mess. I had to adapt a standard of excellence before I could expect excellence from my team. God was truly preparing me for a major promotion, and I had no idea.

Remember: The way you do *anything* is the way you do *everything*.

Your personal standard of excellence is all about preparation for something greater. Pastor Steven Furtick says, "What's *next* in your life is always connected to what's *now*."

God is watching, observing, and noticing how you care for the little things in your life. When He sees someone paying attention to details such as picking up trash off the floor rather than walking over it, putting things back where they belong rather than leaving them out for someone else to pick up, or hanging things back rather than leaving them on the floor, He is getting ready to promote!

In fact, the Bible says that Daniel became distinguished

above all other high officials because "an *excellent spirit* was in him" (Daniel 6:3, ESV, emphasis mine). His personal standard of excellence brought him from the lowest to one of the highest positions in society back then.

Daniel wasn't just your average Joe working an average job. He was a slave! He wasn't married, didn't have any kids, he had nothing. He wasn't someone being groomed for success or to be in the public eye. Daniel was the lowest ranking guy on the totem pole, so-to-speak, but God's favor was on him. Why? Simply because he had an excellent spirit. He was actually promoted as the head over three presidents and in charge of overseeing the king's financial affairs. Think about that: A slave had oversight of the king's money!

Scripture says, "Daniel was preferred above the presidents and princes..."[3] The word *preferred* means to be handpicked, approved, favored, adopted, liked and endorsed! Your standard of excellence can pave the way for you to be promoted when you seem to be the least-likely, the last choice, the shock of the season to those around you. It will cause you to be set apart and promoted above all others who may even be more qualified, educated, and experienced than you!

Excellence opens doors in your life that no man can shut! Excellence puts you on a path for success.

Purge. Prepare. Perfect.

After I heard that first directive to get cleaned up in 2002, I saw God drastically promote my life and ministry and began doing things I had only dreamed of. I went from ghostwriting books to authoring books, from attending conferences to speaking at conferences, from watching television for hours to co-hosting a

TV show. My marriage was completely healed and restored, my finances drastically increased, and my ministry was launched and began growing tremendously each year. And then the Word of the Lord came again!

One morning in 2014, I heard these three P's in my prayer time: Purge. Prepare. Perfect. Again, I wasn't real clear on what the Lord meant by that instruction, but I took it literally. Although my home was not in the poor condition it had been in years prior, it had accumulated clutter. Little by little, junk had been piling up in closets and cabinets. So, I started again by making a list of each room and what needed to be done to purge it, perfect it or make it excellent. I defined what purging and perfecting meant to me: condense, eliminate, stack, fold, give, trash, reduce!

For example, I had numerous coats hanging in the closet that I rarely ever wore. I had unused Christmas gifts piled in the guest room closet for years. Beach towels from 1995 (frayed and somewhat painful to use) stuffed in cabinets with beach balls and swim shoes. Light bulbs that had burned out months ago in rooms rarely used so they were ignored. A broken doorknob on the back door to the garage. Scuff marks all over the hardwood stairs. Perfume jars (with maybe one squirt left in them) taking up space on my bathroom vanity. Eyeshadow, old mascara tubes, trial-size shampoo bottles from hotels, and nail polish bottles that would only paint four fingernails!

I had become clutter-blind!!

I clearly mapped out what needed to be done to make each room in the house excellent.

It's amazing how we can get blinded to clutter, adjusted to junk, and acclimated to debris. We get so used to things that once irritated us, but as time goes by, we ignore it and don't even notice it anymore. When you imagine your house being on the market to sell and potential buyers touring your home, it gives you an entirely new perspective.

I devoted a little bit of time each day to this purge, prepare, and perfect directive. Little did I know, three months later, God would instruct me to not only put my house up for sale (which I had no intention of doing) but to also resign my position as the CEO (where I had been promoted 11 years prior), move to a new city, and start my own organization from scratch. Again, without my knowledge, this attention to excellence was another preparation for promotion.

Once the home was in excellent condition, we sold it, moved to another city, launched the organization, and God has far exceeded my greatest expectations! The growth, the increase, and the favor of God has been unprecedented. I am convinced that purging, preparing, and perfecting the little things in my life were a prerequisite.

Second Timothy 2:21 says, "If a man therefore purge himself from these, he shall be a vessel unto honour, sanctified, and meet for the master's use, and prepared unto every good work" (KJV, emphasis added). This encourages us to be prepared by excelling, clearing the clutter, and getting things in order.

Many times we want to see promotion immediately, but excellence takes time. In fact, all great things take time. Remember, in my first story of being told to "clean up and clean out," I did get promoted, but it was nine months later. For three quarters of the year, I had to maintain that cleanliness and organization in my home before God could trust me with oversight of a worldwide ministry.

When we don't see the results we desire overnight, we tend to quit and revert to our old ways of doing things. Keep in mind, your Father who sees what is done in secret will reward you in the open (Matthew 6:4).

Every time you make the bed in the morning, knowing full well you're going to crawl back in that evening, you're preparing for promotion.

Each evening that you load the dishwasher before going to bed so you wake up with a clean, orderly kitchen, you're preparing for promotion.

Each time you hang your clothes up rather than leave them on the floor to pile up, you're preparing for promotion. You might think, "This is ridiculous! I could care less about this stuff." I can't stress enough that it's these little habits and personal standards that truly enable us to soar to new heights.

God sees everything. He sees every time you pick up the piece of clothing that falls off the rack at the department store and hang it back up (rather than walk over it). He sees every time you put the ketchup back on the shelf with the other condiments when you realize you don't need more (rather than hiding it with the detergent because you're too lazy to go put it back). He sees every time you put the toilet paper back on the roll (when the rest of the family just stacks it on top of the empty one). He is watching and observing every act of excellence, and when He sees this lifestyle exemplified in you, get ready, major promotion is headed your way!

Always remember, "Whatever you do, do it all for the glory of God" (1 Corinthians 10:31). God is watching, observing, and eagerly waiting to promote a person of excellence. So, let's purge ahead and whip things into shape.

Chapter 2

The 10 Benefits of Getting Organized

Let ALL things be done decently and in order.
1 Corinthians 14:40

US News and World Report shared an alarming statistic that the average American spends one year of their life looking for lost or misplaced items.[4] What could you do with an extra 365 days added to your life? Seriously consider what clutter and chaos are costing you. Think of the progress you could make writing that book, launching that ministry, starting that business, losing that weight, getting that degree, learning that second language, traveling the world, volunteering at that safe house. Instead, you're searching for the remote control...for a year!

The average American home has 300,000 items in it.[5] At the same time, 80% of what we have, we never use.[6] I want you to see how a little bit of time wasted each day by having clutter and being disorganized can add up quickly to missing major opportunities in our lives.

Newsweek magazine discovered that we are wasting an

average of 55 minutes a day (approximately 12 days a year) looking for things we own but can't find.[7] Nearly two weeks of our lives each year is dwindled away, never to be regained, due to our clutter and lack of being organized.

We are inundated with paper and junk mail; in fact, on average we receive 49,060 pieces of mail in our lifetime and one-third of it is junk.[8] Each year, about 100 million households receive 16.6 billion catalogs.[9] When the catalogs arrive, they just go in the pile adding to the overall feeling of clutter, confusion and chaos in our environment.

Getting organized is consistently one of the top five New Year's resolutions year after year, but 80% of people say at any given time their house is a mess! If most people fail in the area of clutter clean out and getting organized, then why even put forth all this effort? What's in it for you to get your house cleaned up, tidy and in shape?

Let me share with you the 10 benefits of this process so you'll realize at the onset that your organizing efforts far outweigh the exertion to get going.

1. You'll save money. Instead of buying things you already have (i.e. AA batteries, soap, glue, scissors, socks, light bulbs, cleaning supplies, etc.), you will know exactly where to locate them and save money you don't need to spend. *The Wall Street Journal* reported that simply buying duplicate or last-minute supplies due to disorganization can cost a business up to 20% of the annual purchasing budget. We don't realize the money we are wasting by running up to the store each time we can't locate the batteries. By getting things in order, you might even find the coupons you misplaced and you'll really save money!

The 10 Benefits of Getting Organized

You'll eliminate excess money flying out the door by having your bills organized properly which will ensure they are all always paid on time. Twenty-three percent of adults pay bills late and incur late fees because they simply can't find them.[10]

Disorganization is a drain on your wallet.

When you're organized and clutter-free, you won't need to rent a storage unit to house your excess belongings because you'll only keep what you really need. Self-storage spaces have become a $154 billion industry with one in eleven Americans renting these units and spending on average $1,000 each year to store their clutter.[11] Think of what you can do with an extra grand in your hand!

In addition to saving money, you could actually earn income by selling things you don't need (see Chapter 7).

2. You Can Find Things. Have you lost your keys or your cell phone again? On average, we are spending six minutes a day just looking for our car keys in the morning! I read where the top five items men look for in their homes are: clean socks, the remote control, wedding album, car keys, and their driver's license. (Although, I have no idea why men would be searching for their wedding album unless it's just to remind themselves of the approaching anniversary date.)

How about for women? Do these top five items women search for sound familiar? Shoes, a child's toy, wallet, lipstick, and the remote control.[12]

With a clean home, you'll designate specific spots for every item, and you'll know exactly where to look when you need it. You will go directly to the key hook for your car keys, to the coat closet for your jacket, to the file cabinet for your insurance card, and to the laundry room for your flashlight.

You'll have such a sense of peace when your home is in order and everything is in its rightful place.

3. You'll save time. The average American woman spends 55.2 minutes a day looking for lost or misplaced items.[13] That's nearly an hour a day wasted! As I mentioned before, that's approximately two weeks squandered a year due to disorganization. Imagine what you could do with an extra half month this year!

IKEA reported a statistic showing that women with shoe racks are seven times more likely to be on time for work than women without shoe racks.[14] If your shoes always go in the closet on the rack (I know it's crazy), you won't be running all over the house searching for them. If your cell phone, purse, wallet, bills, magazines, jackets have designated spots, you won't waste valuable time hunting them down.

The average executive wastes six weeks annually searching for important documents lost in the clutter.[15] That's over a month of productivity gone! In fact, 43% of Americans surveyed described themselves as disorganized and 21% said they have missed crucial work deadlines because of it. Nearly half said disorganization causes them to work late at least two to three times a week.[16]

Forty percent of adults say that if they had more time, they would spend it with family,[17] but what we don't realize is, according to cleaning professionals, getting rid of clutter could cut cleaning time as much as 40%. Look at the hours we can gain and spend with our families by getting things in shape.

4. You can be more creative. Having an orderly, clean space allows your mind to relax and be more focused and productive.

The 10 Benefits of Getting Organized

When your area is in shape, your brain doesn't have to work so hard. Your mind is sharp, your concentration is focused and the order around you feels good inside.

On the contrary, when your surroundings display uncleanliness and disorganization, your thoughts will focus more on the chaos around you than the creative ideas you want to develop. Clutter truly is an "inside job" affecting your mental health and ability to create. It ruins your concentration and draws your attention away from what's important to you. It's a constant "should be doing" thought hanging over your head.

Keeping your environment clean and tidy will help you welcome tranquility. T.L. Osborne said, "Tranquility produces creativity."

5. Your life will be less stressed. How often has the stress in your life been related to a messy environment or disorganized space? Your mood is affected by your surroundings. According to The Centers for Disease Control, 80% of our medical expenditures are stress related.[18]

One of the most life-changing, therapeutic, peace-producing tasks you can pursue is to create a clutter-free environment around you.

Ninety percent of Americans say disorganization at home or work has a negative impact on their lives. Sixty-five percent say clutter affects their state of mind. Fifty-three percent say it reduces motivation and forty percent say it leaves them feeling unhappy.[19]

It's peaceful when you know where things are. If you could find everything you needed when you needed it, imagine how less complicated your life would be. In fact, scientific studies have linked clutter and disorganization to depression and anxiety. Messy rooms, misplacing items, being late and missing appointments are all huge contributors to anxiety and stress that stem from being disorganized.

Organizing experts have even reported their clients have lost weight, ended toxic relationships, left unhealthy jobs and stopped bad habits once they decluttered their lives. Clearing your space clears up your mind as well.

6. You'll sleep better. We spend one-third of our lives in the bedroom, which is more time spent in any other room in the house. This room is designed for rest, relaxation and sleep. Studies show that people with clutter in the bedroom experience more sleep disturbances.

There's nothing more irritating and distracting than focusing your eyes on the overwhelming disorder in your bedroom as the last thing you see when you turn off the lights and the first thing they focus on as you awaken the next day. Whether we are consciously aware of it or not, it can weigh on you all night interfering with your sleep. Physical clutter in your surroundings overloads your senses preventing you from experiencing the best rest.

There's nothing more peaceful than climbing into bed with clean sheets, warm blankets and drifting off to sleep in a tidy bedroom. Imagine the floors vacuumed or mopped, the clothes folded in the dresser, the nightstand cleared of clutter and the soft aroma of fresh lavender calming your mind and senses.

Your mind will rest at ease knowing your home is as it should be. You won't be waking up to chaos or drifting off to disorder. With a sleep-friendly environment, you'll improve the quality of your rest which will improve the quality of your life.

7. You'll have more time and energy to go after your dreams and goals. When your home is dirty or disorganized, it's difficult to focus on the bigger tasks you should be doing. When everything is organized, your bills are paid on time, your laundry is sorted and done, your meals are planned, and your papers are filed, what are you going to do with all this extra time? Start the workout, paint the room, take the cooking class, learn the foreign language, write the book, research the business, attend seminars, start reading a book each month.

When you're not always feeling the pressure of needing to get that room cleaned up, you can focus your time and energy on the bigger goals of life—not the maintenance of life. Your mind is free to plan other things.

8. You'll be a great example for your family. Your children and family are watching, observing, and learning from you every day. Showing them how to keep things clutter-free and organized will prepare them tremendously for the rest of their lives. It reduces stress, anxiety, and chaos in their lives when your home is in order.

In addition to the excellent example you set, it improves the overall health of you and your family. It's not good for anyone to live in clutter and filth, but especially small children. As babies crawl around on a dirty floor, they can be susceptible to germs and bacteria that affect their health. As you keep your home sanitized and clean, your entire family will be healthier.

9. You'll build better relationships. In a survey conducted by NAPO, 1,397 people were asked, "How long would it take you to get your house ready for dinner guests?" Sixty-five percent said four hours or less; 11% said they would never invite anyone inside; 10% said eight hours; 7% said 24 hours and 6% said 40 or more hours![20]

It is so embarrassing to have unexpected guests show up at your house when it's messy and disorganized. When this repeatedly happens, you tend to not invite anyone over. Don't allow a messy home to prevent you from spending time with the people you love. When you desire to have friends over but the overwhelming thought of needing to get the entire house in shape stops you, your relationships may grow weaker over time.

Your home does not have to be in museum-like form to be presentable or host your best friends, but keeping things clean and clutter-free can be managed. You'll enjoy telling friends to just pop over tonight when you feel good about the condition of your house.

10. You'll have more confidence. UCLA's Center on Everyday Lives and Families (CELF) explored the relationship of 32 families and the thousands of objects in their homes to conclude that clutter has a strong effect on moods and overall self-esteem.[21] Women, especially, feel embarrassed, ashamed and guilty with the presence of clutter.

You just feel better about yourself when things are in order. You may not have control over every situation in your life, but you do have control over the condition of your home and your space. When you organize your home (to your personal standard), you will feel more competent, in control, and empowered. Getting your house in shape will improve your self-esteem and self-image. You develop confidence in "your castle." Your home truly becomes your haven.

The 10 Benefits of Getting Organized

As you can see, the little inconveniences of cleaning are worth it in the long run when it produces a checklist of benefits causing you to feel happier, healthier, and possibly even wealthier. So, let's get started creating calm, functional spaces that make you feel both energized and more relaxed.

Chapter 3

The Laundry Basket Law of Success

Clutter is not a stuff problem; it's a behavior problem.
Deane Alban

Back in the early 1970's when my parents were starting their journey of serving God and being in full-time ministry, my dad was traveling nonstop and my mom stayed at home with my sister and me. My parents barely had any money and were trusting God to pay every bill. They were living in a house that was in such bad shape it was about to be condemned. They were driving an old car with well over 100,000 miles on it and my mom was wearing cut down maternity dresses from having me two years prior. They were living by faith on a daily basis, trusting God to provide.

One typical day, my mom was going about her daily household chores of doing laundry, cooking, cleaning dishes, and caring for two small children. As she collected the clothing from the dryer and routinely did what she always did—toss them onto the

guest room bed until time to wear something from the pile—
she heard this phrase in her spirit: *Finish your laundry.*

"What? What was that? Who was that?"

She heard it again, so softly in her heart: *Finish your laundry.*
Then, she heard this phrase going over and over inside: *Finish
what you start, and take care of what you've got, and God will
bless you with better.*

God was teaching her a lesson. I like to call it the "Laundry
Basket Law of Success."

In other words, she was learning to apply Matthew 25:21,
"You have been faithful with a few things (the laundry); I will
put you in charge of many things (a global ministry)" (additions
mine). *The New American Standard* says, "Because you were
loyal with small things, I will let you care for much greater
things."

God showed her that she had not finished the laundry
simply because the clothes and towels were thrown on a bed
and remained there until time to pull something out of the
wrinkled pile and put it on. That wasn't *caring* for small things.
That wasn't finishing what she started. She learned these basic
and seemingly petty things. Wash, dry, fold, and put away the
laundry. Finish what you start. She learned to iron her old
maternity dresses, hang them up, wear them with dignity, and
thank God for them. She learned to fold the towels and put them
away in the bathroom cabinet until it was time to wrap up in
them.

He began to teach her that she hadn't finished the dishes
simply because they were left in the dishwasher until time to pull
them out and eat off them again. They were finished once they
were dried and put back in the cabinet where they belonged. He
was teaching her to establish standards of excellence with the

little that she had so He *could* bless her with more.

She learned to empty the car out of all the trash built up and the crumbs on the floor. She wiped down the dashboard and vacuumed the seats of that clunker. She learned to make the beds each day without fail, to vacuum that worn carpet and clean those old linoleum floors. She was preparing to be trusted with greater *things* (towels, clothing, dishes, cars, houses, etc.).

God was watching, observing, and eager to promote her. As she practiced this habit day after day, week after week, God began trusting her with those nicer things. She began to do away with re-shaped maternity dresses and purchased new, flattering dresses. She acquired finer towels, prettier dishes, newer carpet, which eventually led to driving a luxury car and living in a bigger, nicer house. God began to prosper and promote my parents in ways they only dreamed of as they began placing significant importance on "finishing what they started and taking care of what they had."

You could be dreaming about having a new car. Maybe you even have a photo of it on your vision board. However, the one you're driving is full of fast food trash, mud stains on the floor boards, with lining ripped out from the ceiling, and hasn't been washed in months. You've got paragraphs written all over the windows, "Please, for the Love of God, wash me!" Maybe it's not in that bad of shape, but it's not excellent or presentable enough to offer your boss a ride to lunch in.

My recommendation for you is this: Get that car cleaned up and act as if it were a brand new BMW. That's being loyal with small things. Treat it with honor and make it as nice as it can be. Get the inspection sticker renewed. Vacuum the floor. Empty the trash every time you stop to fill up with gas. Wipe down the seats and the dashboard. Clean off the steering wheel. Organize the glove compartment. Throw away the old insurance cards. When God sees how you care for this vehicle He has entrusted you with (for this season of your life), He can determine whether you can be trusted with something nicer. Show Him you are trustworthy and capable of overseeing much greater things.

Successful People are Organized

If you know anything about me, you know that I am passionate about teaching you to have a vision. Proverbs 29:18 says, "Where there is no vision, the people perish" (KJV). Well, I remember when I was a little girl, my dad was pastoring a local church in Fort Worth, Texas. There was a family who had a dream of owning a brand-new Cadillac.

This particular family was clear on their vision, and they continually told my dad, "We are declaring that we have a brand-new Cadillac, debt-free, in Jesus' Name!" I'm also passionate about making faith-filled declarations over my dreams and goals. Finally, one day, my dad said, "Let me go see the car you're driving." They walked him out to the parking lot and at one glance anyone could see why they were not driving a brand-new Cadillac debt-free no matter how clear the vision was or how consistent their declarations were.

The current car they were driving was absolutely filthy. It looked like something from a junkyard. My dad was honest with them and said, "God is not going to bless you with a better car when you don't take care of the car you've got." He said, "Act as if this car were the Cadillac. Show God that you can be trusted with a nicer vehicle." He went on to say, "If you don't take care of this car, give it a few months, your Cadillac will look just like this!" I hate to say that I never saw them acquire that new Cadillac, but I also never saw them clean up their car.

Bottom line: God won't bless us with *more* when we're not faithful with *little*. If you're believing God for a new car, a new job, a new house, a new ministry, or a new career, one of the greatest strategies for success is to act as if you already have what you want to have. Practice excellence now on the way to where you desire to be.

Excellence is one of the character traits of God. Genesis 1:31 says, "And God saw all that He had made and it was very good." Notice it doesn't say, "And God saw all that He had made and that it was *average*." Or, "God saw all that He had made and that it was *acceptable* or *mediocre*." No, it was very good.

We should look at our surroundings, our work, our home, our pantries, our closets, our cars, our endeavors and have that same sentiment, *it is very good.*

A Lifestyle of Excellence Opens Paths to Success

Radio host Dennis Rainey said, "Many are on a *career* path, but few seem to be on a *character* path. All too frequently who we are is discarded upon the altar of ambition. Today our oatmeal is ready to eat in 60 seconds, our prescription lenses are ready to be picked up in 60 minutes, and our house can be built in 60 days. We are a culture that is used to getting what we want instantly. We aren't used to working patiently, or waiting on anything—even a hamburger."[22]

Isn't that the truth? That's why Jesus taught in Luke 16, "He who is faithful in a very little thing is faithful also in much; and he who is unrighteous in a very little thing is unrighteous also in much. Therefore if you have not been faithful in the use of unrighteous wealth, who will entrust the true riches to you?" (vs. 10-11, NASB).

Even Joyce Meyer illustrates how God couldn't release her ministry to the world until she got victory over a sink full of dirty dishes. She had to take care of what she had at home and finish what she started before she could televise her broadcast across the globe.

She goes as far as to say that God dealt with her for *years* about putting her grocery cart back in its marked spot rather than leaving it situated up against the curb, the sidewalk or another car (with the potential to roll into another vehicle). This wasn't a one-time lesson for her; she routinely had to be corrected to put the cart where it belonged. When she finally got the lesson ingrained, she was able to move on to bigger and better responsibilities. I certainly don't want to be held back for years while God is trying to teach me one simple lesson of excellence.

Dennis Rainey goes on to say, "What we want today is the *much more* without the *very little*. We want the tip without the toil, the gain without the grind, the sweets without the sweat, the prize without the pain, and the perks without the perseverance. Today, duty, diligence, hard work, and attention to details are a rare commodity in any endeavor—whether it be at home, at work, or at church."

You strategically put yourself in position to increase by being faithful with the material things God has given you.

For example, if you're renting a house and you desire to have a house of your own, take great care of that rental house and treat it as if it belongs to you. Don't stain the carpet or bang up the walls unless you replace it or repaint it. Don't be careless with it. Jesus said, "If you have not been trustworthy with someone

The Laundry Basket Law of Success

else's property, who will give you property of your own?" (Luke 16:12).

Gloria Copeland said, "God gives us certain responsibilities in His kingdom. He gives us assignments. Our first assignment might be nothing more than to weed the flower bed at the church or to wait tables at a restaurant. But if we'll be faithful over that assignment, the next assignment He gives us will be bigger and better."

Up to now, you may have never been told these things, but you can start developing this standard in your life today. God always rewards excellence. These are small areas that God is watching, observing and eagerly looking to promote.

Nothing is so fatiguing as the eternal
hanging on of an uncompleted task.
William James

My mom's personal lesson in success was a two-step formula: (1) Take care of what you have, and (2) Finish what you start. We saw from the Word of God how important it is that we care for the seemingly small things in our lives in order to be blessed with greater things, but the other side of that formula—finish what you start—has a profound effect on our emotions.

When projects go unfinished, not only do they take up physical space but they also take up mental space. When you have that nagging feeling inside that you need to clean up that bathroom, fold those clothes, finish paying those bills, take out that trash, paint that room, or load that dishwasher; it is taking up mental space in your mind. Why? Because it's not finished.

Not only am I referring to the things you should be doing around the house, but also the things you should be doing in life and keep postponing such as: the oil change in the car, the dentist appointment, opening the savings account, redeeming gift cards, using frequent flier miles, filing taxes, returning the clothing you changed your mind about, repairing the broken printer, etc. All your unfinished projects and messes are draining your energy and stealing your peace.

When you procrastinate in the small areas of life (paying bills, loading the dishwasher, returning phone calls, getting check-ups, etc.), it can trickle over into the bigger areas of life (getting the Master's degree, getting the life insurance policy, writing the book, launching the ministry, etc.). In the next chapter, we are going to address procrastination with a 30-day Knock It Out Challenge to get you motivated and moving towards your promotion!

Tomorrow is the only day of the year that appeals to a lazy man.
Jimmy Lyons

Chapter 4

What Does Your Space Say About You?

Closets can be a window into people's mental health.
Melinda Beck[23]

There is a story about a guy who was considering renting a house so he scheduled a tour with the landlord. As he pulled up to the property, he was greeted curbside by the owner, but before she commenced the tour of the home, she began oddly asking him one question after another about his car. "How long have you had it? How do you like it? Does it drive well?" You might assume it was a foreign luxury car, but it was an economic Honda Accord. Finally, after all the inquiry and interest in the vehicle, she decided to give him a tour of the house.

After seeing the home, he was sure it was a perfect fit for him so he asked the landlord, "Have you had a lot of interest in the house?" She responded, "Yes, I have shown this place to several people, but quite honestly, you are the only person I would consider renting it to."

The renter was puzzled and asked, "Why was I the only person to make the cut?" She replied, "You are the only person that I have showed this place to that keeps their car clean and tidy. From experience, I know if someone takes good care of their car, chances are they will take care of my rental." That afternoon, he signed the lease.[24]

Your organization or disorganization says a lot about you and often determines the opportunities you are given.

> *By their fruits you will know them.*
> **Matthew 7:16 NKJV**

Your outer world is a reflection of your inner world. Best-selling author, Brian Tracy said, "The car you drive and the condition that you keep it in will correspond to your state of mind at any given time. When you are feeling positive and confident and in control of your life, your home, your car and your workplace will tend to be well-organized and efficient. When you feel overwhelmed with work, or frustrated and unhappy, your car, your workplace, your home, even your closets will tend to reflect this state of disarray and confusion. Everything is from the inner to the outer."[25]

Psychologists believe that our homes mirror our emotional state. If your items are always lost, perhaps you feel lost in life. If your house feels out of control, perhaps your life feels out of control. If you're always overwhelmed with how much to clean, perhaps you're overwhelmed with how much to do.

When your surroundings are out of order, it causes you to feel less productive and less energetic. It has a way of draining you of motivation. It's hard for our minds to feel at ease when things are messy all around us. You tend to feel guilty for working on your big dreams and goals because you know you should be getting things cleaned up; therefore, your mind isn't free to be productive. Clutter makes it difficult for you to relax fully because of all the constant reminders staring at you.

One example I've read says that clutter competes for our attention in the same way a toddler might stand next to you annoyingly repeating, "Candy, candy, candy, candy, candy, candy, candy..." This article went on to say, "Even though you might be able to focus a little, you're still aware that a screaming toddler is also vying for your attention. The annoyance also wears down your mental resources, and you're more likely to become frustrated."[26]

An Inside Job

Many people only think of clutter as having too much stuff, but clutter is anything you're keeping around that doesn't add value to your life. A mess is any disagreement between the way you desire things to be and the way they actually are. That's a lot more than just having stuff around the house. And that mess causes stress. Hazel Thornton, owner of Organized for Life, said, "There's no one who calls me who isn't stressed out, frustrated or feeling inadequate, incompetent in their job, or guilty. It's all about emotions—definitely it's more about emotions than it is about the stuff."[27]

Those who live in a constant state of being overwhelmed feel anxiety and stress with how far they have to go to get things in order, so they continue to put it off, therefore, maintaining a lack of confidence and peace. If you're not looking after the clutter in your home, you may not be fully looking after yourself either.

"I feel like if I could just get rid of all this clutter, I could go on to do great things." One woman told the professional organizer, Jennifer Hunter, whom she had hired to declutter her things.

"Maybe that's why you keep the clutter," said Hunter, without hesitation.

The woman was shocked and defensive. Surely, she wasn't insinuating that her disorganization and clutter was some sort of internal excuse for underachieving in life! Or maybe it was.

Professional organizers agree that they witness the emotional rewards as well as the physical ones when getting a home in order. Jennifer Hunter goes so far as to describe the job as "Halfway between a therapist and a housekeeper."

She explains, "Clutter matters because it takes up space— not just in your surroundings, but in your head. Of the two, the psychological effect of clutter is the most important."

As a professional in her field, she has heard her clients breathe a sigh of relief when the clutter is cleared. The mood, the atmosphere, the emotional state changes instantly. People feel calm, refreshed, more focused and lighter. It's as if a heaviness has lifted inside and out. "The effect is profound," says Hunter.[28]

All that stuff you've collected over the years has emotional baggage attached to it. That's why you've been holding on to those "skinny" clothes even after they went out of style, because tossing them could signify you failed (again) at reaching your weight loss goals.

We save movie tickets, concert t-shirts, love letters, and childhood crafts out of sentimental value. Perhaps we fear trashing these objects would mean we would forget the good times they represent. It's one thing to have memorabilia from the past, but making a temple of nostalgia from the good ol' days is another.

What Does Your Space Say About You?

I loved when my daughter Kassidi would come home from school with another piece of artwork, but if I had kept every picture she drew me, I wouldn't have room for anything new! If you're still holding on to every piece of artwork from your child (who is now collecting artwork from their child), it might be time to purge a few drawings.

When your surroundings are infused with memories of the past, you tend to remain in the past. You are prone to keep looking back rather than focusing forward on the new things God has for you.

You may have items that are holding you back emotionally, but you have no idea what a negative toll it is taking on you. In my book, *Untangle*, I deal with this topic in detail relating to relationships. Sentimental items from a former love, photos that conjure up painful memories from an ex-spouse, gifts from former friends, clothing with bad memories attached to them. Any items that conjure up uncomfortable emotions should be marked for removal. It will be challenging, I'll admit, but the rewards of freedom are priceless.

When we clear the clutter, we are not erasing the memories. Holding on means not letting go. God has so much more for your life. You haven't seen your best days yet, but your clutter could be preventing you from recognizing the new things awaiting you.

Clutter Matters

Your home should reflect a place of comfort, but comfort and clutter do not go together. A recent survey discovered that one-third of respondents admitted they avoided spending time at home so they didn't have to deal with their mess.

Declutter Your Way To Success

No matter how much or how little, your clutter does more than just get in the way. It's a mindset that paralyzes you from moving forward and making progress in having an organized life. It can weigh you down so heavily that it welcomes chaos into your life and causes you to miss out on promotions God wants to give you.

In Rick Renner's book, *Ten Guidelines to Help You Achieve Your Long-Awaited PROMOTION!*, he bluntly states, "How a person treats his home usually reveals to you how he will treat your church, ministry or organization. The care of his home reveals his attention to details, his standard of excellence, the pride he has in the way he lives, and the high or low level of respect he has for himself." Renner continues, "I am so convinced of this that before I place someone in a top leadership position on our team, I pay a visit to his house—unannounced."

He goes on to say, "People can only impart what they have in their own personal lives. If they don't have a needed quality at home, they probably can't give it to the organization either." Our surroundings speak volumes to other people.

There is a direct link between organization and success. The organization of your surroundings reflects the organization of your life. To put it mildly, *clutter blocks success*! Where there's clutter in your home, there will be a degree of clutter in you.

Keep in mind, that everyone's idea of a clean, clutter-free and organized home will be different. Don't feel guilty about what you decide is best for you. The goal here is to create order, tranquility and new behavior patterns that lead you to a more productive, rewarding life.

Julie Morgenstern, author *Organizing from the Inside Out*, believes that if you can find what you need when you need it, you're happy with your space, and you don't feel like your

What Does Your Space Say About You?

clutter is getting in your way, then you are sufficiently well-organized. However, if you are ashamed, embarrassed, feel guilty and avoid time at home, these are indicators that your clutter needs to be cleared out and put in order.

> *Your environment often perfectly mirrors*
> *many of the other situations in your life.*
> **Jack Canfield**

Stop Putting Off the Little Messes

Remember, the way you do anything is the way you do everything. In other words, if your bed is always half made, perhaps your book will remain half written.

We discovered in chapter 3 how your messes and unfinished projects (or incompletes) wear you down and prevent you from reaching your important goals! Jack Canfield teaches in his bestselling book *The Success Principles* that we must clean up our little messes before we can start to excel in our lives.

What are these little messes? It's the broken doorknob that you complain about month after month but do nothing to fix it. It's the stain on the carpet that you are bothered by walking passed every day, but you don't replace it. It's the jam-packed coat closet that frustrates you every morning when you grab your jacket, but you have no plan to organize it. You don't realize you think much about it, but it's there. It's there just enough to drain your energy and steal your peace.

When you have all these unfinished projects and little messes around you, it weighs on you internally. You feel guilty about working toward your big goals when you should be finishing all these little incompletes in your life.

The act of continually putting things off and delaying action is procrastination. Not many of us want to admit that we are procrastinators. Yet a shocking 95% of us procrastinate at some point,[29] and 20% of the world's population are *chronic* procrastinators.[30]

There is an emotional toll that accompanies procrastination. It produces feelings of being incompetent, incapable of accomplishing things, annoyed, depressed, anxious, lethargic, unmotivated, and overwhelmed. That does not sound like a person prepared for promotion.

Our procrastination effects those around us as well. It inconveniences others, annoys our friends and family, and leaves us feeling embarrassed and ashamed.

Let me boil down the extensive research I've read on the matter and say it this way: Procrastinators are *less wealthy, less healthy* and *less happy* than those who don't delay.

Procrastination is just another way you will avoid fulfilling your dreams and goals. It's time to conquer the procrastination once and for all! So, let's attack it with a plan!

Knock It Out!

As you're reading this chapter, I hope you are thinking of the areas in your life where you have put off taking action. Where do you feel out of control? With the information you have read, take a look at the accumulation of stuff around you. What does it tell you about yourself? Where have you taken in or taken on too much stuff? Why do you believe you have all these objects collecting space around you? The thought of it might fill your mind with dread and anxiety, but it's time to address these issues, put an end to the nagging incompletes in your mind, and gain intense focus about the most important areas of your life.

In the *Declutter Your Way to Success* companion workbook, there's a place for you to make a list of the top 10 things you've been putting off. Really think about it. For example, if you need to have a health check-up but have procrastinated for months, write it down. It could be major or minor things such as: repair the kitchen faucet, replace the printer, change the light bulb in the bathroom, get the car inspected, return the phone call, finish painting the guest bedroom, go to the dentist, return the clothes, file the bills, etc.

After you make your list, I want you to attack it with a 30-Day Knock It Out Challenge! Look on your calendar over the next thirty days, and schedule each task, one-by-one, over the next month. You may be able to complete a few tasks in a single day. Determine to follow through and then, check it off. Trust me, you will feel exhilarated! You'll wonder why you procrastinated for so long, and it will build your self-esteem as you begin pursuing your bigger goals.

Finishing what you start and taking care of what you have will cause you to present yourself with a good image, not a disheveled mess. You will gain respect from others simply due to your attention to excellence in your environment. Rather than feel the drain of a visual mess, you'll embrace the energy to enjoy your life. Instead of feeling out of control and overwhelmed, you'll put yourself in the driver's seat of life, ready to move full speed ahead into the dreams and goals that need your time and attention.

Don't let the small things in life cloud out and obscure the bigger things in your heart to do. Develop that mental force inside that refuses to delay another day ignoring the issues around you. Give yourself the gift of completion by following through with your decision.

Remember, the Laundry Basket Law of Success says: *Finish what you start*, take care of what you've got, and God will bless you with better.

> *Only put off until tomorrow what you are*
> *willing to die having left undone.*
> **Pablo Picasso**

Note: Some people have extreme emotional and/or sentimental attachments to things and can become hoarders. In some instances, they are afraid of letting go of things because what they have is all they have. In other words, they fear having nothing. In severe cases, a counselor needs to address these emotional attachments so they can truly experience the freedom Jesus died to give them.

Chapter 5

Are You Clutter-Blind?

Every step towards order brings you peace.
David Crank

Many of us realize we have too much stuff. However, we tend to think if we only had more *space*, then we could be better organized. According to The National Soap and Detergent Association (yes, there is such a thing), statistics prove that 80% of household clutter is the result of disorganization, not a lack of space.[31]

Read these startling statistics, obtained from Joshua Becker at Becoming Minimalist, proving our need to purge our possessions a bit:

- There are 300,000 items in the average American home, but the average size of the American home has nearly tripled in size over the past 50 years. And yet, one out of every ten Americans rent offsite storage units to house their extra possessions.

Declutter Your Way To Success

- The average 10-year-old owns 238 toys but only plays with 12 daily.
- The average American family spends $1,700 on clothes annually, but throws away 65 pounds of clothes annually.
- Nearly half of American households don't save any money, but they spend more money on shoes, jewelry and watches ($100 billion) than on higher education.
- American homes have more television sets than people, and the TV is turned on for more than a third of the day (8 hours 14 minutes).
- Shopping malls outnumber high schools, and 93% of teenage girls rank shopping as their favorite pastime.
- Women will spend more than 8 years of their life shopping.
- Americans spend $1.2 trillion annually on nonessential goods—in other words, items they do not need.
- The $8 billion home organization industry has more than doubled in size since the early 2000's and is growing at a staggering rate of 10% each year.[32]

In other words, we like stuff! At the same time, all these objects piled up around us are negatively affecting our productivity, time, budgets and mental health.

Let me ask you, has the clutter been there for so long that you don't even notice it anymore? Have you become oblivious to it? We can get so acclimated to our disorganized living spaces that we just walk over it day after day. What used to annoy us to no end has now become invisible. Just as some people are color-blind, we become clutter-blind.

Let me point out that there are different degrees of clutter that are unique to each person. What one person considers orderly, another considers a catastrophe. And they tend to

40

marry each other! In fact, I have had many people ask me out of curiosity, "Does anything get you upset?" I do have an easy-going personality, and I don't get disturbed or agitated by much. However, I can identify the main thing that ruffles my feathers or as I like to say, "steals my peace" more than anything else. It's coming home to a messy, cluttered, disorganized home.

In the past, there were many times when I would arrive home late at night from traveling all weekend speaking at conferences, and as soon as I would walk in the back door, I would be greeted by empty pizza boxes stacked on the kitchen counter, dishes piled in the sink, coats hanging across chairs, and backpacks on the table. I would gasp in disgust and could hardly even drop my luggage from my arm before I was grabbing a trash bag to dispose of the cardboard pizza boxes! That is not a good way for me to return from a trip with the best attitude for my family.

Being married for 26 years now, my husband knows how important a clutter-free kitchen is to my arrival that he consistently makes sure I return to a house in order. It makes me happier than I can express to see dishes put away, countertops wiped clean, and a birthday cake-scented candle burning. In fact, I'll text him when I get on the plane to alert him of my arrival time and I'll ask, "What are you doing?" Knowing I'm en route, he typically responds, "Making peace for you." How I love him!

We all have different tolerance levels for disorganization and clutter (mine and Rodney's are completely different), and the person with the lowest tolerance level will end up doing most of the work to get things in shape.

Some people have no qualms about leaving their dirty clothes on the bathroom floor for a solid week or walking over a pile of laundry for several days (okay, maybe I'm referring to Rodney, maybe not).

Declutter Your Way To Success

In fact, I read a story about a woman whose husband was so messy that she wanted to do a little experiment just to see how long he would go without noticing clutter. When they returned from a trip, she left his suitcase full of dirty clothes right by the front door. He literally had to step over it to get in the house. After a solid month, she called off the experiment and emptied the suitcase!

It may not be totally fair that one spouse has to maintain most of the order, and do most of the tidying up. In most cases, the less tolerant spouse isn't trying to be rude or disrespectful; the mess just does not bother them. They don't even see what you see. That's when you have to hold on to the scriptures that say: Do everything as unto the Lord. Make the bed, pick up their underwear, do the laundry, load the dishwasher, clean the bathtub, file the bills....as unto the Lord. Why? Because your Father in Heaven is watching and He sees every act as a preparation for promotion. All those tedious acts in private will bring rewards to you in public.

Even if you are the more organized one in the family, you can still become oblivious to some of the clutter built up (in hall closets, junk drawers, nightstands, garages, pantries, dresser drawers, etc.). The longer we live in a situation, the less able we are to see it from an outsider's position. Sometimes you simply need a little change in your perspective to see what needs a fresh, clean sweep.

We get so accustomed to how we live and our current standard that it's difficult to see the need for change...unless you imagine your boss coming over for dinner tonight! Now you may see things in a new light. Imagine your domain from his/her viewpoint of walking in the front door. Would you be ashamed, embarrassed, mortified, or completely content and proud to

42

show off your aptly presented castle? Only you can decide, but changing your perspective can really open your eyes to what must happen to give you that sense of pride in your place.

What exactly is clutter? It is the accumulation of things that impede your ability to feel relaxed, at peace and confident about your living space. It's when you can't fully rest in your haven because your home has evolved into a never-ending to-do list in your head that constantly nags at you. This removal and clearing out will help you find what you need when you need it, allow you to fully enjoy your living quarters, and give your mind rest from the overwhelming feeling that clutter produces.

You've heard the scenario of "if your house were on fire, what would you grab?" This question could help you determine how much you need, value, and love an item, or if it's time to kiss it goodbye.

Before you grab your broom and dustpan, you need a plan. Many people get excited about the vision of a clutter-free, organized home but get quickly tripped up by the next question: Where in the world do I start?

Everything starts with a vision. Before you tackle any room or area, let's start by getting a vision of what needs to be done room-by-room. You start with one room, one section at a time. Once you get a plan to get organized and get things in order in your home, you'll probably discover you actually have more free space than you ever thought. We'll establish that plan later in this chapter.

The Urge to Purge

Purging is therapeutic. In fact, Colleen Madsen at 365 Less Things gives away one item each day all year long. She reports having felt quite a transformation by reducing her stuff one day at a time. To purge means to clear or get rid of an unwanted feeling, memory or condition, or to physically remove something completely. Let's develop the urge to purge and remove anything that could be dragging you backward so you can be free to move forward.

Here are some decluttering tips that organizing experts recommend. Read each one to see which of them you identify with as being a good strategy to get you going.

The twelve-month rule. Many professional organizers suggest this tactic to making strides in your clutter-free home. One of the biggest reasons we accumulate so much stuff is because we have so many old items that haven't been used in years. It could be due to fond memories or an "I may need it one day" mindset. If you haven't needed it or used it in the past year, the general rule is to toss it or give it to someone who will appreciate it and even utilize it.

Something old/Something new. When it comes to clothing, research shows that we only wear about 10-20% of our items hanging in our closet about 80% of the time. (I'm pretty sure I wear more than that!) The point being, do we really need so many clothes if we aren't even wearing them? It's recommended to separate your newer garments from your older ones and then consider blessing someone in need. The problem with overstuffed closets is that we love to obtain more and more new articles of clothing without ever ridding ourselves of anything. The closet becomes more and more crammed with shirts stuffed, wrinkled, and packed to capacity making us feel overwhelmed just getting ready each morning.

Are You Clutter-Blind?

Many decluttering experts recommend you only give yourself permission to purchase an item if you remove a similar item. If your closet is already overstuffed, remove a pair of shoes before you add another pair. For everything you buy, you must remove a similar item. If you buy a new set of Tupperware, remove the old Tupperware with lost lids! As you buy something new, consider removing something old. Your old item could be something new to someone else.

The "Do It Now" process. When you take your clothes off at the end of the day, complete the ritual by either putting them in the dirty clothes hamper or hanging them back up. It's a one-step process when you follow up immediately. Otherwise, you throw them on the floor or across a chair only to be attended to at another time. Do it now.

It's the same with dishes. Don't stack dishes in the sink after dinner. You're making things harder on yourself by having to return to that chore later and tidy up. Load plates in the dishwasher as soon as you finish dinner. It's done. Don't create extra steps for yourself that only welcome that overwhelming feeling of so much to do. Do it now.

When you bring the stack of mail in from the mailbox, immediately toss the junk mail in the trashcan and sort the bills to be placed in the spot marked for bills. Don't store the junk mail only to be sorted through again. Do it now. This behavior will instantly reduce clutter (and stress) build up.

Sarah Felton calls it the "30-Second Rule," (not to be confused with the "Five-Second Rule" of eating food dropped on the ground if it's been there for five seconds or less!). This rule implies that if a job takes around 30 seconds or less to do, do it immediately. Put the shoes away, throw the junk mail in the trash, carry the towels from the laundry room to the bathroom. Do it now.

Stop the junk. One simple way to cut down on paper clutter is to cancel the junk mail from being delivered to your mailbox altogether. The National Association of Professional Organizers discovered that the average American receives nearly 15,000 pieces of junk mail in their lifetime. How much of it is lying on your kitchen counter right now? Eliminate this whole process by canceling the mail from being sent. There are many websites that can give you tips on how to do this, including www. consumer.ftc.gov or ecocycle.org.[33]

Go paperless. Avoid the whole mail process altogether by going paperless and having your bills electronically emailed. It not only eliminates the paper cluttering, but it saves you time by not having to open each bill one by one and sort through them.

Automate your bills. You may have reduced the clutter by filing the bills and even going paperless, but if you want to simplify your life even more, have your bills set up for payment automatically. The quickest and easiest way to organize your bills is to set up the automatic draft from your checking account to the bill collector. You can do this with everything from your electric bill, your gym membership, your savings plan, and your phone bill.

Consolidate. Do you really need seven frying pans? Or 32 cleaning products? What about 17 tubes of lipstick piled in a drawer and 27 pairs of socks with 11 mismatched? We tend to unconsciously collect too many items that can simply be merged, condensed, and even tossed to free up more space. If you discover that you have too many of an item, purge it!

Take the 30-day Decluttering Challenge. This is an activity that many who are considered minimalists have employed into their lifestyle of living with fewer material possessions for the purpose of finding more freedom in life. (Note: I am not advocating or opposing this lifestyle. I am simply promoting a clutter-free, peaceful environment.) The challenge is to simply remove one item each day that corresponds with the day of the month. For example, on the first day of the month, you remove or declutter one item from your possessions. On day five, you remove five items that have no use to you. On day fifteen, you declutter fifteen items that are taking up space in your surroundings. By day thirty of this decluttering challenge, you will have removed 500 unnecessary items from your domain! That's major progress and a little fun in the process.

Make a Plan

Are you ready to make a clean start on decluttering, getting organized and preparing for your promotion? Follow these steps as a guideline:

1. Write the vision.

Before you get started, make a plan. Take a walk through your home with the companion workbook (or simply grab a paper) and write your vision for each room. This is your written plan for how you want each room to look when it is done, and a detailed list of what needs to be cleaned out to meet that vision. Focus on one room only and begin making a list of *every single thing* that needs to be done in that room alone. It can be as menial as, "Master Bedroom List: put shoes in closet, hang coat, trash the newspapers, remove the pile of books, clean off nightstand, vacuum floor, open curtains."

You might think you're finished, but let's keep going. After you write down what can be seen at a glance, let's go deeper. It could be: wash sheets, organize each drawer in the dresser, declutter nightstand, empty trash. Go ahead and list the things that only you know need to be organized and cleaned up. Believe me, tackling this one room and making it a masterpiece is going to give you such a boost of confidence, you'll be motivated to go after the others with gusto!

After you have made the list (and you still have not picked up one single item), let's move to the next room and write every single thing down that needs to be done. Make this room-by-room checklist first. Trust me, you will be glad you did.

2. Start with one room.

How do you know which room to start decluttering and organizing? It's simple. Start with the room you spend the most time in. You need this constant reminder of completion and accomplishment, so attack it first. Choose a room that doesn't contain a great deal of sentimental items so you can make great progress at the onset. The more you clear out some space, the more motivated you'll become.

Whatever room the family seems to congregate in the most, start with that room. It could be the kitchen, family room, game room, home office, etc. Don't select the guest bedroom that you hardly ever visit or the garage that stays closed and never used.

You need to see your progress immediately to stay motivated to keep going.

Grab your workbook and follow the vision you wrote for this room. Focus your efforts on this one room until your vision is complete, then move on to the next.

3. Start with what's visible.

Before you begin cleaning out the refrigerator, the kitchen pantry or the spice rack, always begin with the clutter that can be seen. If you decided to start your organizing in the kitchen area, start by loading the dishes piled up in the sink. Place all food left on the counter back in the pantry or refrigerator. Wipe off the counter tops. Place the pile of bills in the home office or kitchen desk. Take the shoes to the closet and the newspapers to the trash. Clear off all visible messes first and foremost.

4. Designate a category for each item.

Use these four categories to sort your stuff: (1) Trash, (2) Give, (3) Keep, (4) Sell. As you set out to declutter each room, locate four boxes (or large trash bags) designated to one of these four categories. Categorizing will help you with the decision-making process. Don't get too caught up in the sentimental value behind each piece. The goal is to create a sense of tranquility and self-esteem in your surroundings. We're after progress!

It could be random items such as:

- unused kitchen utensils/appliances (tourist mugs, the blender from your wedding 17 years ago, broken cheese grater, rusted cookie sheets, Easter bunny Jell-O molds, etc.)
- unused Christmas gifts (the rotating necktie organizer, the 5th foot massager, another flashlight, blankets, the

PedEgg, etc.)
- broken items (lamps, clocks, tools, etc.)
- stored furniture (all the stuff that keeps getting moved to the garage)
- junk (anything taking up space that you have no need for)
- negative memories (any item that has a negative emotional attachment or brings up old memories that you have no need in rehearsing, trash it!). It's not easy, but it's liberating!

How to determine which category each item belongs in:

Trash: If it's broken, missing a piece or unusable, it's time to dump it. Just get rid of it. It is taking up unnecessary, valuable space, and it will benefit you more by being out of your way. If it's outdated, worn out, stretched out and faded, toss it. It could be a broken toaster, a Sony Walkman from 1997, old newspapers and gossip magazines. Nobody cares anymore what happened in 2003. We care about a sense of peace and tranquility in your living space, so just shred it!

Give: It's rewarding to give to someone else. You may have too many of a particular item such as coats, umbrellas, old phones, shoes, jewelry, dishes, Tupperware, etc., and you could be a tremendous blessing by donating these items to someone in need. God always rewards a generous heart. Proactively look for opportunities to be a blessing to someone else by seeking out items to give away (and clear up some much-needed space in the process).

Keep: As you come across items, ask yourself when was the last time you used this, wore this, or needed this item? Most organizing experts say if you come across something you haven't used in the last 6-12 months, you should probably get rid of it.

A neat trick that organizers teach with clothing, books, DVDs is whenever you use an item over the course of a year, place it back facing the opposite direction of the others. It allows you to see what you've used and what you haven't. If a year goes by and it's still unused, get rid of it.

Ask yourself if you really love it. If you absolutely love this item, then by all means, keep it. If you wonder why you even bought it, move it out.

Sell: You can really cash in on your clutter. My daughter, Kassidi, was looking for opportunities to make some extra cash and began selling some of her clothing, shoes, purses and costume jewelry on an online used-clothing site, and she has literally made thousands of dollars! I'll share more ideas about how to get cash for your "trash" in chapter 7.

Once you make the decision which category an item falls into, finish the task. In other words, load up the box (or bag) marked "Give" and put it in the back of your car to donate as soon as possible. Don't leave it in a corner of the bedroom for another two weeks or forget about it in the back of your car. If it's marked "Trash," then go ahead and take it to the curb or in the garage until trash day. You have already done so much work to get organized, so now you need to complete the process by following up immediately.

5. Everything needs a home.

Now that we have answered the question, "Does it stay or does it go?", we need to know if it stays, *where* does it go? This is one of the biggest challenges in organization. The reason things pile up is simply because we don't have a designated spot for them. When someone asks, "Where does this go?" if the response is, "Your guess is as good as mine," then it's time to assign a home.

Most clutter accumulates in areas near the main door. We leave things setting out "until I have more time." But we rarely have more time so it just piles up or it all gets dumped in another cluttered area (the junk drawer, the junk closet, the garage, etc.). You must find a place for everything. Everything means the unopened mail, the stacks of photos, the magazines, the photo albums, the unused Christmas gifts, the umbrellas, etc. (See Chapter 8 for some ideas).

You cannot be vague or indecisive about this. Everything must have a place. You must assign a specific place for each item brought into your home.

For example:
- coats in a designated coat closet
- keys hanging on a hook by the door
- cell phones on the charger by the nightstand
- bills in a box on the desk
- newspapers in a basket by the couch
- umbrellas in the coat closet
- purses on the shelf
- backpacks in the hallway bench
- briefcases in the home office
- school information in the desk tray
- coupons in the index box

6. Set your timer for 20 minutes and go full speed ahead.

Are You Clutter-Blind?

You will be surprised at what you can accomplish with a 20-minute plan. What's 20 minutes of your 24-hour day if it produces calmness, peace and a welcoming environment for your friends and family? If your time is limited, then stick to the 20-minute plan. If you can allot more time, two or three hours at most, then set a goal to see how much you can accomplish by focusing solely on this one room today.

As with most of our wishful thinking goals, we choose to put off the attainment of these goals because we are constantly waiting for when we have extra time. Keep in mind, there is no such thing as extra time. You will not have any more time than you already have right now. You must make time.

I always suggest refraining from waiting until you have a full day to organize or an extra hour to clean. Instead, set your alarm for 20 minutes and see what you can accomplish in this burst of time. You will be amazed at how much you achieve.

For example, not too long ago I dreaded opening my makeup drawer each morning because of how much junk had accumulated. Old eye shadow palettes, dried up mascara tubes, outdated lip liners. It annoyed me each day because I love order and organization, but I also love makeup. I kept thinking, "When I have a day at home, I'm going to tackle this drawer." It's rare that I have a full day at home, so I finally set aside 20 minutes to clean it and see how far I could get. It only took 12 minutes!

Many people try to set aside an entire day for organizing the whole house. It drains their energy, causes them to get burned out from exhaustion, and sets them back to where they started. It's more motivating to set aside small sessions of time to declutter than trying to attack it all at once. Decluttering takes more focus, energy, and concentration than most realize. So, set the timer for 20 minutes and just get started. If you're motivated to set another 20-minute timer, then go for it. Hey, 20 minutes over the course of a month is 10 hours of getting your home in shape!

7. Add the final touch of excellence.

When you clear out the clutter and get a room in order, don't just stop there. Make it excellent. Once things are no longer taking up space, it's time to vacuum, mop, dust, spray, and shine the room. I love to finish it off by either lighting a candle or using a plug-in air freshener to give it that look and smell of completion and sparkle.

Let me remind you that we are striving for excellence not perfectionism. Even the best professional organizers will tell you that after they have added their magical touch to a formerly cluttered closet, it hardly looks like the ads for The Container Store. It will look miles better, more efficient, and neat, but closets being used by humans are far different than advertisements staged by stylists.

8. Don't break the chain.

Stephen Covey said, "Don't prioritize your schedule; schedule your priorities." Priorities never stay put. I want to motivate you to develop a routine of cleaning and getting organized by scheduling at least a 20-minute regimen every single day for 30 days. And then vow to keep your appointment with yourself.

The great motivator, Zig Ziglar, said when he was a salesman that he had never even been in the top 5,000 in his sales company, but he made a commitment to be successful. He made a vow to go to work on a regular schedule and believe in himself. At exactly 9:00 every morning, without fail, rain or shine, cold or hot, he was committed to be out knocking on somebody's door. The amazing thing is that his wife would ask him, "Where are you going?" And he would always say, "I've got an appointment." He never told her his appointment was with himself to be knocking on those doors. The year he kept his commitments, he finished second place out of 7,000 salespeople.

I am fond of citing Habakkuk 2:2, "Write the vision, make it plain," in reference to the powerful necessity of having your dreams and goals penned on paper. Habakkuk 2:3 says, "For the vision is yet for an appointed time." You must appoint a time to go after your vision of having a clean, organized, clutter-free home. In addition to this powerful success key, it's extremely motivating to see your discipline practiced over a period of time by using a wall calendar in a prominent place. Each day that you follow through with decluttering, cleaning or organizing your home, you get to place a big X over that day.

In fact, one of the most successful comedians of all-time, Jerry Seinfeld, co-writer of the long-running sitcom *Seinfeld*, uses this strategy with enormous success. His awards, earnings and creative comedic gift is impressive, but what's most intriguing about Jerry Seinfeld is his remarkable consistency and discipline.

When Brad Isaac was just getting his start out on the comedy circuit, he met Seinfeld backstage and asked for any tips for a young comic. Seinfeld told him the way to be a better comic was to create better jokes and the way to create better jokes was to write every day.

"He told me to get a big wall calendar that has a whole year on one page and hang it on a prominent wall. The next step was to get a big red Magic Marker. He said for each day that I do my task of writing, I get to put a big red X over that day," said Isaac.

Seinfeld said, "After a few days, you'll have a chain. Just keep at it and the chain will grow longer every day. You'll like seeing that chain, especially when you get a few weeks under your belt. Your only job is to not break the chain."

He went on to point out that it didn't matter if Isaac was motivated or not. It didn't matter if he was writing great jokes or not. It didn't matter if what he wrote would ever make it into a show. All that mattered was, "Don't break the chain."[34]

As of 2016, Seinfeld's net worth is over $800 million dollars.[35] He is now regarded as one of the "Top 100 Comedians of All–Time" by Comedy Central. Now that's a guy I want to take productivity advice from.

I want to challenge you the same way in your decluttering habit. Don't break the chain for 30 days straight. In the companion workbook, I've even provided a 30-day calendar for you to mark your chain. Don't break it! After 30 days, hopefully, you will have instilled some new behaviors and habits that you will maintain in your daily life.

Warning: Don't Get Distracted

As you get started, it will be tempting to get distracted by other rooms as you're taking items where they belong. If you find your jogging shoes in the kitchen floor and you take them to the closet where they should be, you may find yourself straightening up all the shoes because you want everything organized now. Before you know it, you have forgotten about the kitchen and left it unfinished because you're disgusted by your closet. But you're exhausted now, and you feel even more frustrated because *everything* is a big cluttered mess! "Thanks a lot, Terri!" you'll say in disgust! I am speaking from experience here. Just put the shoes in the closet, go right back (immediately) to the kitchen, and stay focused. One room at a time is the goal.

Are You Clutter-Blind?

Don't wait for the perfect time to start when you have nothing better to do. That time will never come. This is a vital part of God preparing you for promotion. He wants to see how you care for the personal standard you have in your home. It is proof of how you will care for the next level where He wants to take you. So, don't justify putting it off until you have free time. You won't have any free time to do this; you have to make time. Don't look at the one hour you don't have, look at the 20 minutes you do have, and start today.

Remember, outer order equals inner calm.

Chapter 6

The Financial Cost of Clutter

Have nothing in your house that you do not know to be useful, or believe to be beautiful.
William Morris

When my daughter, Kassidi, was entering kindergarten, we toured several elementary schools to get an idea of what they offered and what would be best for us. I will never forget sitting in the front office waiting to meet with the principal of a nearby private school. When her door swung open for us to enter, I probably gasped out loud!

My eyes locked in on the overwhelming number of textbooks in every corner of her floor and lining the back wall. Magazines were stacked two feet high and falling to the floor. I've never seen so many manila folders piled on top of a filing cabinet in my life. Artwork from students scattered across her credenza. Leftover food sat on her desk. Not to mention the principal's high-heel pumps laying on the floor as well as a pair of house slippers to help her get comfy in that peaceful, little oasis!

Her first remarks to me were, "Please forgive me for the messy office. I apologize for how bad it looks. I'm Principal..."

But I didn't hear much else. My immediate thought was, "If you have to apologize upfront for the condition of your personal work environment (and you are the leader of this institution), then your team will most likely model your behavior (and probably apologize for the condition of the classroom)."

There are no second chances on a first impression, and my first impression was, "If your surroundings are a big mess; perhaps you and your school are a mess as well."

Her desk was so cluttered, she couldn't locate the "New Student Enrollment Packet" so she asked her assistant for a post-it (she couldn't find those either) and wrote down our address to mail us a packet (costing unnecessary postage). I'll be honest, decision-making is not one of my best gifts, but that decision was immediate for me solely based on the disorganization of the principal. If that is the standard she has for herself, that's the standard she will impart in the students.

I knew without hesitation that was not the school for our daughter. The principal's clutter was costly to the academy. Think about it: She lost our tuition as well as any referrals I could have given.

Clutter is expensive. Most of us have clutter in some areas of our lives; in fact, less than 10% of people surveyed say their homes are clutter-free.[36] We don't realize how much clutter could be costing us in our personal and professional lives. In the previous chapters, we have discovered how our lack of order could be causing us to miss out on significant promotions due to messy and disorganized surroundings. But clutter is costing us something constantly, not only in stress and a lack of peace, but also monetarily.

The Financial Cost of Clutter

What Could Clutter Be Costing You?

Depreciating cars. Twenty-five percent of Americans with two-car garages can't even park their cars inside because they are storing other stuff instead. The vehicles develop wear and tear from the outside elements depreciating the value of the car when it's time to sell it. Think about the price of the items stored safely and protected in a covered garage while your costly vehicle is enduring the elements outside.

Late bills and late fees. Twenty-three percent of Americans don't pay their bills on time and incur late fees because they have lost the statements. If you're late on your utility bills, they can shut the power off costing you even more money to reconnect electricity. This expense can show up in other areas like ruined food in the refrigerator or freezer due to the power being off, not to mention damaging your credit score causing you to pay higher interest rates in the future.

Wasted food. You could be wasting food that was overlooked in the messy pantry or the cluttered refrigerator that has since expired and can no longer be used.

Buying duplicate items. If you can't find items because of clutter, you may wind up buying duplicates or even triplicates wasting money you don't need to spend. It could be batteries, light bulbs, glue, scissors, etc.

Eating out too often. If your kitchen counters are too messy to cook on, you may be eating out more than you should for your family budget.

Declutter Your Way To Success

Tax deductions missed. If you're consistently misplacing receipts due to clutter, you could be missing out on tax deductions that could save you thousands of dollars.

Higher mortgage payments. If you have too many (unnecessary) possessions that it caused you to purchase a larger home just to store your things, it is costing you a higher mortgage.

More clothes. You may have bought clothing (maybe even on sale) but can't see the new shirt you bought because it's crammed in so tight with all the others that you forgot about it and ended up buying another one just like it.

More gifts. You might have purchased a gift for a family member but can't remember where you stored it so you had to buy another gift. When you finally locate it, it might be too late to return (or you won't be able to find the receipt).

Reduced sale price of home. Clutter can prevent you from selling your home if you wish to move. Your home will stay on the market much longer than you would like because a cluttered home is an unappealing home. You may even settle on a lower price.

Higher moving costs. Clutter will cost you more to move. The more items you have to carry across town will require larger trucks and more movers to handle it. Aim to declutter before you put your house on the market to increase appeal for a quicker sale.

The Financial Cost of Clutter

Less time to pursue your dreams. I mentioned previously how research proves that if you get rid of the clutter, you can eliminate as much as 40% of the housework in an average home. It's worth it right there! You can free up 40% of your time allocated to housework so you can go after your dreams.

Imagine time available to study the foreign language that will cause your salary to double because you're bilingual. Imagine time available to read books on personal growth that will cause you to be promoted because you're more valuable to your company. Imagine time available to write your manuscript that can be published and change lives (as well as provide additional income). There are endless opportunities to be seized once you get your life in order. Don't miss out on the productive pursuits that await you!

Stress-related costs. As we have discussed, clutter produces depression, anxiety and stress. When you experience these symptoms, you may call in sick, miss more work days, and need medical treatment resulting in more doctor's bills and prescription fees.

Storage fees. I mentioned earlier that statistics show nearly 10% of American households rent storage units to house their excess belongings. They are spending more than $1,000 annually in these rentals. Imagine doing that for the next ten years. That adds up to $10,000 wasted to simply keep your clutter that you're not using and don't miss. Most of the time, we don't even remember what we stored. What if you used that money towards your family vacation, emergency savings or retirement investment? Just think about it. I asked a professional investor, Adam, to give me an example of investing $1,000 per year over a 10-year period with 12% ROI, and he showed me a client whose portfolio grew to $17,558! You could potentially have over $17,000 if you part with those stowed away possessions![37]

I do not mean to imply that everything in your storage unit is junk, but only you can evaluate whether or not the stuff being stored is valuable enough to outweigh the cost of investing that money.

How about at work? What is all this clutter at our jobs costing us? For example, at the office, are you able to locate the document your boss wants immediately? If not, it may cost you a valuable promotion. Have you or your team missed a conference, banquet or event due to misplacing an important invitation? What could that have done for your business had you been there? New relationships, connections, new business.

Research shows that 80% of items that are stored in a filing cabinet or stacked on your desk will never be read, seen or dealt with again. It's just taking up space physically and mentally. In a shocking study by Brother International, U.S. corporations lose $177 billion annually due to clutter![38] It's hard to wrap your mind around. So, we could take a tip from The Productivity Pro, Laura Stack, and declutter our workspace by only using three folders: to read, to do, and to file.

Somebody once said that having excess clutter is like having a slow leak that can cost up to hundreds or even thousands of dollars every year. Everything from late fees, bank fees, expired gift cards, unnecessary storage units, missed appointments, and cancellation fees are all adding up and draining your wallet. Not to mention the doctor appointments and medication needed to cope with all the stress that clutter is producing. The good news is clutter is completely within your control.

It might be somewhat daunting and depressing to go through

room-by-room and take an inventory of what all your clutter is costing you, but it will create peace in your life, your home and your office space. That is worth it!

In the next chapter, I am going to show you how to cash in on this clutter and make a dent in your belongings and benefit your billfold.

Chapter 7

Turn Clutter into Cash

The wise have wealth and luxury, but fools spend whatever they get.
Proverbs 21:20, NLT

We have discussed how costly clutter can be in wasting your valuable resources month after month, but now it's time to profit from your possessions. Why not gather together the stuff you collected in your Sell box or bag from chapter 5, assess what you have, and see how you can turn that clutter into cash!

Nearly half of employees in a survey said that saving more money is their top resolution this year,[39] yet 69% of Americans have less than $1,000 set aside.[40] This chapter will offer you many ways to continue the path of your cleaning spree while reaching a financial goal in the process. We discovered that Americans like their storage units and are spending $20 billion per year to store their excess items[41] that are depreciating as time goes by. There is no use holding onto these items when you could be putting money in your pocket.

Declutter Your Way To Success

According to a survey conducted by eBay, the average household has more than 50 unused items worth roughly $3,100 in their homes.[42] What could you do with an extra $3,000? That's some good motivation! You can get some cold hard cash for your trash. The Italian Rosetta Stone that's unopened in the closet. The digital photo frame never loaded with photos. The outdated iPod you never use. The Bowflex machine sitting in the garage. The stationary bike that's remained stationary. It's true that one man's trash may be another man's treasure.

Once you've launched into the decluttering process full speed ahead, set a 30-day goal to get it out of your house. Keep the time frame short or you'll begin to feel like your home has turned into a flea market rather than an oasis of peace. Sell everything you can as quickly as you can, and consider donating the rest. After all, a man's harvest in life depends entirely upon the seeds that he sows (Galatians 6:9, Phillips).

Set a financial goal that you want to reach as you monetize your clutter. The point is not to trade your stuff for more stuff; it's to organize your space and profit in the process. Imagine raising $1,000, $3,000 or $5,000 allowing you to make a significant dent in your credit card debt, vehicle payoff, college tuition, family vacation, or emergency savings account.

Keep in mind as you declutter, this is not just about unwanted items, it is unused items as well. How many items have you shoved to the back of the closet thinking, "What if I need it someday? You never know. It may come in handy—even though it hasn't for the past 10 years!" There's no reason to accumulate or hold on to things that you don't use, don't plan to use, don't need and don't really love.

Turn Clutter Into Cash

Ways to Cash in On Your Clutter

Local online sites. These local online sites such as Craig's List are especially good for larger items that would be difficult to ship. The couch you need to sell, the old refrigerator, the kid's bikes they outgrew, the washer and dryer are just taking up space and preventing you from cushioning that emergency savings account. Research shows the trend leans towards making more money selling these large items on local online websites than having a garage sale. (We'll talk about garage sales further down.) Always be careful, as with anything on the Internet, when dealing with and meeting people you don't know. Be sure to safeguard yourself by using protected payment systems and watching out for scams.

Global online sites. There are so many sites out there ready and willing to sell your items for you with a global audience. Amazon Marketplace, Etsy, eBay, etc. Many of them are simple to set up so you can start advertising goods that are no longer useful to you but irresistible to someone else.

Garage sale. This is the old go-to when you're in the mood to get things out of the house quickly and don't mind discounting prices for those hardcore garage sale goers. You won't get top dollar, but you can move a lot of stuff in a single day. Advertising is key in having a successful garage sale. It's pointless to sell your wonderful objects if nobody knows you're having a sale. Yard signs will alert neighbors, but online ads or posts on the Yard Sale Treasure Map app will draw the attention of those not already passing through your neighborhood.

Price everything simply to save time. Rather than place a

tag on each item of clothing, generalize all shirts, pants, shorts, tops, etc. for one single price. You can group items together to increase a single purchase such as: All shirts $3.00 each or 5 for $10. It eliminates some of the haggling, encourages more purchases, and moves your clutter out of the garage.

Find out if your town or community is planning a neighborhood garage sale to increase your potential shoppers and profits.

Consignment shops. These are great for barely worn designer clothes or trendy, brand-name pieces of clothing, as well as furniture you paid good money for. There are several consignment shops that focus on baby and children's clothing, as well as video games and toys. Wash and iron your pieces to make them presentable and irresistible to consign. You should expect to see your item on display for sale at a price much higher than they will be paying you. They require a certain amount to help you sell your stuff. The benefit of a consignment shop is that you earn more money for valuable pieces rather than bottom dollar at a garage sale, you simply drop off the piece, and let them do the work. That alone is worth splitting the profits!

Auctions. Did you get into collecting action figures in the 1970's? What about those Wheaties cereal boxes with the 1984 Olympic gymnastics team on the front side of the box? Baseball cards? Barbie dolls from the 1960's? If you really want to declutter and earn some cash, here's another way to fill your pockets.

If you truly possess some unique and rare items that others may find of great value, you could consider selling them at an auction. They tend to be up-to-speed on the value of collector's items and unique finds. You can visit a local auction house or visit an online site to get an idea of what your piece is valued at.

Antique store. If you have something that has been passed down from relatives and you no longer have space for it or any emotional attachment to it, then you could consider approaching a local antique shop. Some antique shops rent out space for you to display an array of vintage pieces, others may purchase it from you outright knowing it has potential to sell, and other antique stores will do business like a consignment shop advertising your item until it sells and taking their commission as a fee for selling it for you.

Pawn shops. Your local pawn shop can provide quick cash on items that are in good condition such as jewelry, musical instruments, sports equipment, etc.

Facebook pages. If you don't feel comfortable selling to perfect strangers, you could consider advertising to your friends on Facebook. Using social media as your network to reduce clutter is free, and you will be dealing with people you already know. There are also Facebook groups for buying, selling and trading items. Search for local groups near you and post your items for sale.

Donate. You can generate some cash indirectly by donating your items. If you donate certain items to a nonprofit organization, you'll receive a tax write-off that can help you with your itemized deductions when filing taxes.

Declutter Your Way To Success

A Few Tips Before You Sell

Do a little research. If you have higher priced items, you need to know the value before you begin posting online. You can get a pretty accurate figure for what your items are worth by visiting websites such as Sage BlueBook for electronics. Type in what you want to sell, and it will research other sites for you while comparing your item to let you know the average going rate. You can decide if it's worth it or not to sell. You can also use eBay's app and bar code scanner to get an estimated value of your item.

Price your items right. After you have completed your research, be sure to price your item to sell. Be honest about its actual condition.

When selling online, list your items properly. Include words like "brand new," "in box," "never opened," and "factory sealed." Use language and phrases that pertain to your item (type, size, color, etc.). Give a detailed description using proper grammar and honesty. Also, a good picture can make all the difference in getting a buyer.

Be aware of prime time posting. Research the best time to post in your area. Studies show that prime times for listing auctions is generally between 7 p.m. to 9 p.m. (CST) to maximize bids and higher sales prices.

Items Worth Cashing in On

Gift cards. If your birthday or holiday included stocking up on gift cards more than cash, then you may want to trade them in for some much-needed money. According to sites such as Gift Card Granny, you can sell them for up to 93.4% of the value of the gift card. It is estimated that the gift card industry is around $124 billion (at this time) with approximately $750 million dollars in gift cards going unredeemed each year! That's hard to wrap your mind around, but I know I've wasted a few. There are several sites you can sell those unwanted, unused gift cards back (depending on the demand of the card), and earn up to 90% or more on the value like Raise.com and Cardpool.com.[43]

Books, DVDs, CDs. Clear your shelves of all those novels taking up space and collecting dust. Local used bookstores will pay you a fee for your media collection. Research online sites who are willing to buy your used games, books and movies such as: SecondSpin.com or Powells.com. You can use Cash4Books.net to sell college textbooks. If you have old movies, books, and CDs stacking up, try Amazon's trade-in program or go to your local bookstore that trades for cash. Even if it's pennies on the dollar, it all adds up and it frees up your space. Other sites to research for selling these items: Half, MyBookBuyer and eBay.[44]

Clothing. If you feel that you don't have time to learn the whole process of selling your items on an online site, managing it, shipping out or meeting with customers, there are many online marketplaces that will do all the work for you. I was contacted by an online clothing store who comes to your house, evaluates your clothing (that you've selected to sell), places them in a large bag, ships them to the headquarters, sells it all for you, and sends you a check. That works for me!

If you do have the time, then selling it yourself will always be more profitable. Research sites that have great reviews and allow you to sell not only designer clothing but that $8.00 t-shirt from Forever 21.

Electronics. Websites like Gazelle.com, Usell.com, BuyBackWorld.com and YouRenew.com (to name a few) allow you to trade in your old electronics such as: iPods, laptops, iPhones, digital cameras, tablets, desktop computers, and other devices. You can browse the value of your particular item by typing in the information, hit return, and see what it's worth.

Ink Cartridges. All those old, used cartridges taking up space in your cabinet can be turned into money. It may not be a lot, but big office supply stores like OfficeMax and Staples will give you store credit for your used ink cartridges in their recycling rewards programs. If you've accumulated quite a few, you can even sell a load of them on eBay for others who may want those supply store credits for themselves.[45]

Furniture. Obviously, the garage sale, the consignment shops, and antique malls are all great for removing those large pieces of furniture taking up space.

Gold. Do you have the old gold chain from the 1980's tangled up in a jewelry case somewhere? What about that ring from Aunt Betsy? There are online sites that allow you to mail in your gold pieces and receive a check; however, you can drive to a local Cash for Gold store and get an estimate in person and perhaps, walk away with cash for that broken clasp.

Refrigerators and A/C's. In some locations, your local

energy company will pick up your old, less efficient refrigerator and carry it off at no cost to you, and give you some cash in return. In addition to removing clutter and earning cash, you will also begin to save more money by using a more up-to-date, efficient model.

Jewelry. Don't mourn over the break-up; grin over the profit. There are even some jewelry websites (such as Neverlikeditanyway.com or IdoNowIDont.com) that will help you benefit from all the unwanted rings, lockets and necklaces you no longer want around your neck. (On some sites you may have to pay a fee and tell your break-up story).

Musical instruments and equipment. Pawn shops and some music stores will purchase your used musical instruments; however, there are certain online sites that will list your item as well. Research which is best for you to get top dollar. Don't just keep Aunt Myrtle's gigantic piano crammed in the foyer with the piano bench used for draping coats across it. If nobody is playing it, remove that elephant of clutter and make some dough.

Groupons. How many times have you bought a Groupon (or from similar discount sites) but never used it? Well, you can sell your unused Groupons on sites such as CoupRecoup, and make some cash. It all adds up.

Rather than dump your stuff off on the curb for the next garbage pick-up, maximize your potential for selling your things and go after those financial goals in the process. The good news is that you will have already created your "To Sell" pile from

Declutter Your Way To Success

each room in the house, so now you just need to name your price and determine your selling strategy. Set a financial target, write it down and keep it before your eyes. It will keep you motivated to move through your pile and fill up your pocket! It's time to not only make room but make money.

Chapter 8

Creative Organizing Ideas

Three Rules of Work: Out of clutter find simplicity;
from discord find harmony; in the middle of difficulty lies
opportunity.
Albert Einstein

It's wonderful to walk into a room that is clutter-free, stream-lined and pristine. However, to create that sense of order, it's vitally important that you create a system that works for you. The goal isn't to make your house untouchable or unlivable; it's to make it functional and excellent. We're after peace, not perfection.

Author Brian Harbour wrote, "Success means being the best. Excellence means being your best. Success, to many, means being better than everyone else. Excellence means being better tomorrow than you were yesterday. Success means exceeding the achievements of other people. Excellence means matching your practice with your potential."[46]

I don't want you to feel the pressure of perfectionism or

compare your standards to someone else's. As a matter of fact, common cleanliness and degrees of organization vary from culture to culture and person to person. You have to find the right routine and organizing method that you can adapt to and maintain. At the same time, I want to push you to come up higher in your cleaning methods and organizing rituals so you're prepared for your promotion.

Jesus was praised for His excellence. Mark 7:37 says, "People were overwhelmed with amazement. 'He has done everything well,' they said." The New Living Translation says, "Everything He does is wonderful." That should be our aim to do everything well and wonderful. Whether it's keeping the car in the best shape we can, putting dishes in the dishwasher immediately after dinner, or making the beds before we run out the door, this standard of excellence means you are doing your best with what you have at this season in your life.

Always remember, "Whatever you do, do it all for the glory of God" (1 Corinthians 10:31). God is watching, observing, and eagerly waiting to promote a person of excellence. So, let's have some fun with these creative ideas.

Before You Get Started

Take before-and-after photos. Everyone loves the big reveal after the work is done. You can motivate your friends to get organized too. Post it on "Transformation Tuesday" through social media and be sure to tag me (@terrisavellefoy). Use the hashtag #iDecluttered so the world can see the new, excellent, orderly you. It will inspire you to tackle the next room, and the next, and the next. The "after" photo will keep you reminded of how it should be maintained weeks from now.

Creative Organizing Ideas

Grow as you go. I always have some sort of motivational teaching playing while I am organizing. It's great multi-tasking. I'm educating myself (which means I'm growing), and I'm organizing at the same time. Get your listening device out and turn it up. Build your faith, learn something new, expand your knowledge or learn a new language while you clean.

Set the alarm for 20 minutes. Set the timer and get started today. Obviously, if you can allot more time to organizing, go for it. But don't stress out over needing an hour to get started!

Random and Creative Organizing Ideas for Every Room

The Entryway, Foyer or Back Door Entrance

These areas are so important to be clutter-free because they are the first impression of the house. Unfortunately, this is where most of the family dumps their belongings. This area of the house sets the tone for what we enter and exit each day. When you walk into an area filled with disarray, junk or filth, it can instantly drain your energy and set a negative tone for the family to endure. An organized, clean entryway makes life peaceful.

- **Umbrellas, backpacks, jackets, etc.**: Turn an average bookcase into an entryway storage locker. Rather than this always being the potential pile-up spot, purchase an inexpensive bookcase (or several if there's room to stand them alongside one another), adjust the shelves to your needs, and add a few hooks to store umbrellas, backpacks, jackets, ballcaps, and shoes. Another idea is use a storage bench to neatly house and hide these belongings. Everything

79

is tucked away inside and the lid is closed. It keeps the area neat and tidy.

- **Newspapers, sports equipment, gloves and scarves**: Purchase bins or baskets and assign one for each family member with their name on it. Store their belongings accordingly each time they enter the house.
- **Car keys, coats, backpacks, dog leashes, etc.**: Attach multipurpose hooks and hanging systems on the back door to neatly hang these items and get them out of the cluttered corner. It reduces time spent searching each morning, and they're easily accessible as you run out the door.

Hint: If the entryway is dark and gloomy, apply a fresh, light-colored coat of paint to brighten up the area and the mood. Add a mirror to the wall to make the area appear larger and brighter, while also giving you that final check of approval before you head out for the day.

The Bathroom

No matter how big or small your bathroom is, there are ways to keep it clutter-free, clean, and functional. In addition to being more attractive and sanitary, a tidy bathroom makes it quicker to get ready in the morning. After you have decluttered this space, it's time to start grouping like items together.

- **Brushes, combs and hair ties**: Your average kitchen utensil tray is perfect for arranging your hair brushes, combs, and all those barrettes and hair ties that easily turn your bathroom drawer into a junk drawer. Rather than only using a utensil tray to sort knives, spoons and forks, you can place your hair essentials in this stream-lined, organized space that typically fits in any average-size drawer.

- **Hair tools**: Use a magazine holder to store your curling irons, flat irons and brushes neatly. You can even display it on the counter top as a decorative piece.
- **Bobby pins**: *Redbook Magazine* recommends a creative way to store all those loose bobby pins by utilizing an empty Tic Tac dispenser. What a unique way to locate those tiny pins immediately.
- **Nail polish**: If you don't want to spend the money on a nail polish shelf, you can use cookie jars purchased from the local dollar store to house your nail polish collection. Or buy several clear cookie jars to group certain colors together. A spice rack is also a good option to store polish neatly away.
- **Lipstick**: Sort your lipsticks and place them in a miniature muffin or loaf pan. (My kitchen items get far more use housing makeup than actually being used in the kitchen!) They make a perfect storage for all those lipstick tubes piling up in a bathroom drawer.
- **Perfumes**: You can enhance your bathroom vanity and save a little extra space by using a 2-tiered cake tray to display your perfumes and lotions.
- **Makeup**: Use your daughter's old bead organizer for your makeup storage. The compartments are just small enough to fit eye shadows and other makeup supplies.
- **Medicine**: Everyone in the family should know exactly where to locate medicine neatly stored in one space in the bathroom. You can mount storage bins to the inside of your cabinet door and place all medicine in one location. It frees up the much-needed medicine cabinet for more of your daily toiletries and necessities. Note: Some experts recommend freeing up bathroom space by storing medicine in the kitchen

area (pantry) due to the negative effect moisture can have on certain prescriptions, plus you probably could use more cabinet space for your toiletries.

- **Cleaning products**: Get a bucket and store all your bathroom cleaning products in one space under the sink. This makes it more efficient to quickly clean sinks, toilets, and bathtubs routinely rather than dreading walking to the laundry room or kitchen sink to find the bathroom products. It's easily accessible and can become part of your nightly ritual.
- **Towels**: Group your towels together by size, color, and sets, then place them neatly folded on shelves or in storage bins or boxes.
- **Vanity**: Keep as few things as necessary on your counter tops. It makes the overall appearance look neater and makes it easier to wipe clean each morning. If your cabinet and drawer space is limited, then display your items with some attractive packaging.

Jewelry

- **Bracelets**: I love the idea of utilizing a paper towel holder to stack bracelets neatly. It allows you to use vertical space and see what you have at a glance.
- **Necklaces**: Reduce tangles and messy piles by purchasing a pegboard, paint it a fun color to your taste, even frame it to make it look even more chic and give each necklace its own hook or nail to hang.
- **Earrings**: Use a simple, inexpensive ice cube tray to house your small earrings and prevent them from getting mixed up.

The Bedroom

Bedrooms seem to acquire a great deal of junk and clutter. The piles of clothes in the corner. The things we don't know where to put so they get stuffed under the bed (only to be forgotten about). The stacks of bills on the nightstand. Old magazines on the floor. Four pairs of shoes by the bed. Since this is where we begin and end our days, it's important to keep it peaceful and tranquil. It can happen with a plan.

- **Extra bed linens or sweaters**: Before you take that old dresser to the curb, use the drawers to place these items in and slide easily under the bed. Purchase footboard storage such as a chest or ottoman that is trendy and chic to add extra storage space to your room.
- **Books, journals, writing supplies**: Choose a nightstand with drawer space if you prefer these items by your bed. It keeps them hidden away rather than piling up next to your head.
- **Books, frames, decorative pieces**: Utilize your wall space by hanging high-up bookshelves for storing your past reads and other things you don't need to access often but don't want to part with.
- **Magazines, work supplies, extra blankets**: If you choose to add an ottoman to the foot of your bed, look for one that has storage availability.
- **Dirty clothes**: If space is limited, you can take advantage of the back of your bedroom door to hang your laundry hamper and get the clothes up off the floor.

The Closet
- **Belts**: A great way to organize your belts is by hanging shower hooks on your closet rod and organizing your belts on the hooks.

- **Clothing**: A good way to utilize limited hanging space in your closet is to attach one hanger to another. You can double the clothing with the same rod space needed.
- **Sweaters**: You can take advantage of those nifty hanging shoe organizers by rolling up your sweaters to fit perfectly in the cubbies as well.
- **Socks, hats, gloves, etc.**: You may think professional organizers have gone bananas on this one, but it works. Buy fruit baskets to hang in your closet to utilize vertical space and keep these small items off the floor.
- **Scarves**: Use shower hooks on a single hanger to display and arrange your favorite scarves in a neat way.
- **Purses**: Use command hooks and hang wire baskets on the back of your closet door to store purses, handbags, extra wallets, and other accessories.
- **Socks, undergarments, etc.**: Use empty shoe boxes to organize your drawers. It makes it easy to locate what you need and prevents these small items from getting lost in the back of the drawer.

The Living Room/Family Room

It's called a living room for a reason. We do most of our living in that space and although it's not difficult to get organized, it's a challenge to keep organized. The best way to keep it organized is by having storage spaces to quickly and easily place things. If your couch offers a console, get into a habit of placing newspapers, remote controls, coasters, etc. in that storage. If you have cabinets, store blankets, pillows and games in a neat, hidden place.

- **Phone chargers and other cords**: I thought this was an

Creative Organizing Ideas

interesting way to keep your loose cords untangled and creatively stored away when needed. Use empty toilet paper rolls to wind your cords down inside. Then stack each toilet paper roll standing up in a drawer. It keeps everything detangled and tucked away.

The Kitchen

- **Soup cans**: Purchase wire baskets and place the cans on their sides. You can stack them easier and keep their labels in sight.
- **Produce:** One organizer suggested repurposing a shower caddy on the side of a cabinet or inside the pantry door to display your onions, peppers, etc.
- **Plastic bags**: We all have those plastic bags from the grocery store crammed in a cabinet or under the kitchen sink, just in case we need them. They take up so much space and never look organized. Try using an empty tissue box to store them inside and easily pull out when you need them.
- **Cutting boards**: Attach a wire bin on the back of your cabinet door to store your different cutting boards rather than taking up space on shelves and inside cabinets.
- **Rice, cereal, and other boxed goods**: You can reduce the storage needed in your pantry by purchasing clear canisters and emptying your cereal boxes into these containers. It frees up space, looks creative, and allows you to see how much of each item is remaining.
- **Sandwich bags, tin foil, and plastic wrap**: You can take advantage of storing these items in a typical cardboard magazine holder. It keeps them straight, organized and easy to grab, plus it stores neatly in the pantry or in a cabinet.
- **Tea bags**: Using your average utensil holder, you can arrange

your creative taste in specialty teas by displaying them neatly in this typical cutlery tray and placed in a kitchen drawer or pantry shelf.

- **Spatulas and other tall utensils**: Utilize the vase that once housed your roses by storing your tall utensils in this beautiful piece and storing it on the counter.
- **Cookie cutters**: Rather than trying to hunt them down each time you decide to make shapes, place them in the cookie jar.
- **Plastic Tupperware lids**: We all have the misplaced and mismatched lids all over the drawers. Attach a metal cooling rack to the top of a basket to line up and organize all those plastic lids. Another idea that seems to be popular is using your old compact disc holder from the 90's to store your plastic lids.
- **Cleaning products**: Install a tension rod under the kitchen sink to hang all the cleaning bottles and free up some cabinet floor space.

The Laundry Room

The key to success in a laundry room is making use of all the space so it's functional, especially if space is limited.

- **Detergent, dryer sheets, bleach**: A hanging storage rack works great if your laundry room doesn't provide cabinets. Install shelves over the washer and dryer to neatly store your supplies while keeping all those extra socks and small articles of clothing from falling behind the appliances. You can even utilize an overlooked storage spot like the back of the laundry room door. Over-the-door shoe systems (shoe organizers) work great for these supplies as well.
- **The ironing board**: Use coat hooks to hide your ironing board behind your laundry room door.

Creative Organizing Ideas

The Play Room

- **Toys**: Lay a bed sheet or large blanket on the floor first before your kids dump all the toys out. When it's time to pick up, just fold the blanket together and place it back in the storage bin.

- **Puzzles**: Get rid of all the boxes taking up so much space and place puzzle pieces in a plastic zip pouch. Be sure to identify it by cutting the box top off and placing it in the pouch.

- **Dolls**: Are you overflowing with little people all over the floor? Use a hanging shoe organizer on the back of a door for storing Barbies and action figures.

- **Stuffed animals**: Use a hammock or a plastic chain hanging from the ceiling with hooks or clothespins to attach each furry creature and get them up off the floor.

- **Books**: Utilize your child's outgrown but adorable wagon to store their books and look cute at the same time.

- **Board games**: If most of the games are no longer played, then turn them into artwork. You can frame some of these colorful pieces and enjoy the fun it produces in the play room.

The Home Office

- **Desk essentials**: The old spice rack has so many untraditional uses. It can also house your office necessities in a creative, cool way to display on your desk. Use individual spice containers for paper clips, thumb tacks, rubber bands, small post-its, etc.

- **Files**: Manilla folders are boring and make it difficult to locate which bill goes in which file. Using a color-coded system allows you to locate what you need at a glance by identifying the color. (Example: green folders for financial papers).

- **Gift wrap**: Pack all those tubes and rolls of wrapping paper in a garment bag and hang it in the guest bedroom closet or hall closet.

The Garage

The craziest thing about a cluttered garage is that most of the stuff taking up the space is worth little compared to the costly car parked out in the driveway because there's no room in the garage. The key to organizing a garage is to tackle it zone-by-zone. Divide it by zones such as: work/tool section, sports (beach balls, tennis rackets, golf clubs, etc.), bikes, lawn furniture, etc. Then declutter each section one-by-one.

- **Nuts and bolts**: A creative way to organize all those little screws and nails getting mixed up in a drawer is (yet again) to use a spice rack to sort them, display them and prevent them from getting mixed up.
- **Small miscellaneous things like rubber bands, pins, nails, tacks, paper clips**: Use an actual muffin pan which provides small compartments for those tiny necessities easily junking up a drawer. It keeps everything stored neatly in its place.
- **Soccer balls, basketballs, beach balls, etc.**: Use bungee cords to corral these items against the wall.
- **Seasonal items**: Use the garage's ceiling space by hanging sturdy racks overhead to place these seasonal items out of the way.
- **Tools, garden hose, etc.**: Purchase a towel bar to contain these items in a neat way by adding a few hooks to hang the tools.

The Car
- **Toys, cups, snacks, etc.**: Put a plastic caddy in your car for all

the miscellaneous things that pile up during your commutes. It will keep things tidy and organized.

- **Hand sanitizer, tissues, snacks, etc.**: Another way to neatly tote your car necessities is to drape plastic or mesh shower pockets on the back of the car's seats for storing small items.

Pick and choose from this variety of organizing tips and tricks to get your home the way you desire it to be.[47] Remember, cleanliness and organization makes you feel good, keeps your mind clear and your concentration sharp, presents an excellent image to those around you, and builds your self-image and confidence. There is a natural connection between the order of your environment and the state of your mind. A pristine, well-organized environment will lift your spirits.

Remember, excellence is a journey, not a destination.

Chapter 9

Organize Your Life

The only difference between a mob and a trained army is organization.
Calvin Coolidge

Work, family, kids, church, school, exercise, sports, goals, relationships, friends, home, pets, personal growth, vacation, sleep...can we really keep all this in balance? I would never say that it is easy. It's not simple to keep everything balanced, and yes, I tend to lean toward the work-aholic side of the scale. But learning to plan effectively helps create more balance.

Sometimes I feel like I'm juggling twelve balls at once between leading an organization, traveling, taping TV broadcasts, writing another book, recording the weekly podcast episodes, speaking at seminars, and oh yeah, the bills need to be filed, the laundry sorted, and the dishes put away! I would never claim to be the epitome of an organized person or that my home is constantly show ready. However, it is important to me to have order and organization in as many areas as possible to maintain my schedule and continue to grow.

I believe a major key to the success I have enjoyed is that I am a planner. An extreme planner. Perhaps I need a little spontaneity in my life, but what gets planned, gets done. The old adage, "Failing to plan is planning to fail" rings true for me. I am a strong advocate of not only planning your dreams and goals, but planning how you'll spend the next hour. Even if you just want to relax, plan it.

The essential foundation of getting organized and prepared for promotion is to have structure in your day-to-day life. I want to share with you how I plan the activities of my daily schedule to keep my life on track. I hope that this will help you get as many areas of your life organized as you can. Everything from your pantry to your purse, from your bills to your bathroom. You will be able to take on more of the assignments God has for your life when you get these areas under control.

How Organized is Organized?

How organized must you be? When do you know you are organized enough? Do your clothes need to be hung according to color or books shelved alphabetically? Must every minute be scheduled and accounted for in a calendar somewhere? And what are the most important areas of life for getting organized? Only you can decide what feels comfortable and calming for you personally.

I want to offer some ideas to help you feel more prepared and planned instead of scattered and haphazard. It's entirely up to your preferences of how organized you desire to be. Remember, changing your behavior takes time, so be patient with yourself. The key to getting ahead is getting started.

Organize Your Life

Always plan ahead. It wasn't raining when Noah built the ark.
Richard Cushing

Use one planner/calendar. Focus is the number one key ingredient to achieving your dreams and goals. In order to get focused, you need to get organized. I learned years ago to record or document every single thing in one consistent planner. Organizing expert, Julie Morgenstern, says, "You have one life; you need one planner."[48]

To keep things simple, record every important task, appointment, reminder in one place. Don't use one planner for work, one for personal, one for your kids' agendas, one for your gym workouts, one for meal planning...it's exhausting just trying to locate each one.

Whether it's digital or paper, use what works best for you. Some people need to touch and feel their work. They prefer to hand write appointments and physically check off tasks completed. Others prefer to digitally document every single reminder keeping it neat and clean with no cancellations crossed out. They simply push delete.

Write everything down. Don't rely on memory alone. Making a to-do list at the beginning of every day or week can make you feel more focused and motivated to continue your work. If you make a list of all the things you have to do, no matter how small, you will feel more accomplished when you check those items off your list and move on to the next task. Plus, we just love check marks!

According to Tom C. Corley, author of *Rich Habits*, 81% of the wealthiest people in the world maintain a to-do list, and only 19% of the poor.[49] Habakkuk 2:2 says, "Write the vision and make it plain," this includes your vision for the day, the week, and the month. It's amazing how much time we can waste when we don't have a written plan for our day. It's equally amazing how much money we waste when we don't have a written list for the grocery store. Rather than go down the list and purchase what we need, we tend to grab whatever grabs our attention wasting money and time. Get into a habit of making lists and writing everything down. You will be amazed at your increased productivity.

Practice the Sunday night strategy. Honestly, you can do this any day of the week and any hour, but I always plan my *entire week* out on Sunday night. Even if I'm flying home from a meeting after speaking on a Sunday morning somewhere. I never go to bed Sunday night without planning my entire week. It gives me an overview of exactly what I need to accomplish and how packed my schedule is. I can see immediately if I have time for any lunch appointments, doctor visits, play time, errands, dinners with friends, and downtime. It sets you up to succeed by having your week thought out and organized. You will no longer wake up wondering what the day may bring. You bring it. You arise Monday morning with vision and a plan, ready to succeed on purpose.

Personally, I make two different columns: Business Goals and Personal Goals (just for the week). I begin listing *every single thing* I can think of personally such as: pay bills, sort laundry, call dentist, get car washed, get birthday gift for nephew, return shirt, go to the bank, save an extra $50, research vacations, lunch with Mom and Dad, call Grandma, mani/pedi, etc. It doesn't have to be in chronological order of when I will take action, it just needs to be thought out and written.

Organize Your Life

After I have considered everything in my personal life to be done that week, then I do the same with my business goals for the week. It could include: prepare podcast messages, tape four podcasts, prepare team meeting, have team meeting, review monthly letter, answer emails, sign thank you cards, prepare four TV broadcasts, choose clothes for TV, tape four broadcasts, get notes for weekend conference, etc.

You can start the process this week in the associated pages of the companion workbook by making a list of everything you currently do or are currently responsible for this week such as: laundry, cleaning house, grocery shopping, paying bills, commuting, team meetings, team phone calls, working eight hours, dance lessons, soccer practice, etc. Think of how this applies in your personal and professional life.

This practice alone has enabled me to be much more proactive rather than reactive in my business and personal life. There's hardly a day that I don't achieve what I set out to do because it's thoroughly planned. What gets scheduled gets done.

Plan each day the night before. In addition to the Sunday night strategy, you need an every night strategy where you never go to bed without mapping out the next day. You simply go down your list of goals for the week, and assign a day for each task.

Once you review your to-do list, designate a specific day for each one to ensure it actually gets done. For example: if one of your personal goals for the week is to "Go online to research accounting classes" but you miss this vital step of assigning a day to actually do it, you'll keep skipping right over it. Weeks will go by and you'll still be delaying your goal of getting an accounting degree. You must appoint a time to do it: Tuesday at

Declutter Your Way To Success

12:00 noon. Always follow up with a date and time.

Examples:

Open savings account – Friday on lunch break.

Make hair appointment – Tuesday at 10:00 a.m.

Declutter kitchen – Sunday at 4:00 p.m.

Do laundry – Saturday morning (approx. 8:00 a.m.)

Prioritize your tasks. Put the most important or hardest tasks first. It's better to save the easier or more manageable tasks for the end of the day, when you're more tired and less compelled to pursue something more emotionally or physically draining. If you put off the hard tasks until the last minute, you'll be dreading getting them done all day.

In fact, one of the top five traits of the most successful people in the world is they make their day "top heavy." In other words, they tackle their most challenging, difficult tasks first thing in the morning. Mark Twain said, "Eat a live frog first thing in the morning, and nothing worse will happen to you the rest of the day."

Fast Company said, "We've co-opted Twain's saying to mean, 'Do your biggest tasks first.'"[50] When you start with your biggest task, the rest of the day looks pretty good! Brian Tracy even wrote a bestselling book called, *Eat that Frog* which was all about tackling your least-desirable and most important task first. You're more rested and alert, so confront it first thing.

Years ago, Andrew Carnegie hired a man to help increase productivity in his company. The man took out a sheet of paper and said, "Every day, make a list of your top five priorities you need to work on. Start your day at the top of the list. Don't move down the list until you completed the most important task first. Don't do anything else until it's done. Pay me whatever you think the idea is worth." And he left. Two weeks later, Carnegie sent the man a check for $10,000!

Time yourself. This is a two-step process.

Step 1. Determine how long each task takes. After you see your daily schedule, you need to know approximately how much time is required to realistically complete the task. Many times, we undercalculate the time needed and end up frustrated with how few of our goals were achieved that day. I used to make lists of 87 things to do and only did 19 by the end of the day. Nineteen! That's a lot. But I was frustrated, mad at myself, and feeling unproductive. Why? My list was completely unrealistic. I thought I could write an article in two hours, but once I started timing myself, it was more like four hours. I thought the phone call would take ten minutes, but it was more like thirty minutes.

When I first began to apply this principle of calculating how long each task really takes, it was pretty tedious. After a while, I began to catch on, and it enabled me to make my daily agendas in a practical and possible way. This includes the time it takes to get ready each day, the time to commute, the time to prepare dinner, etc. You may dread this in the beginning, but trust me, it will lead to an extremely productive life.

Step 2. Determine how much time you need to stay focused on a task. Deadlines are motivating, even 20 minute ones. Because we live in such a distraction-filled society, it's a challenge to stay focused on one task for even a half hour without checking our Twitter account, answering texts or looking at photos on Instagram.

Have you ever wondered how much time you waste each day with distractions?

Declutter Your Way To Success

Television:
- Almost every home in the U.S. has a TV; 66% of American homes have three or more TV's.
- On the low end, American's watch 2.8 hours of television each day. That's about 9.1 years of your life by the time you are 60 years old.
- Some studies show Americans watch over six hours per day.
- 63% of the wealthiest people spend less than an hour per day watching TV.

Smart Phone:
- We spend 4.7 hours per day on our phones! We're typically awake 15-17 hours, so we're spending 1/3 of our time on our phones!
- We now spend more time on our phones than our TV's.
- Most people use their phones during commercial breaks while watching TV.

Social Media:
- On average, people in the U.S. check their social media accounts 17 times per day (adults aged 25-54 check more than teenagers).
- American's spend an average of 3.2 hours per day on social media sites (Instagram, Twitter, Pinterest, Facebook, etc.).

What could we accomplish by eliminating one hour each day from social media/TV/phones? When it comes to organizing your life, you need deadlines to stay focused. Give yourself 20 minutes to work on a certain task without any distractions—without even getting up. When 20 minutes passes, check your phone or social media, go to the restroom, respond to the text, grab a bite to eat. Then, do it again! Set the timer for 20 minutes and get productive.

Create a routine. Keep in mind, getting organized is a lot like eating well and being in shape, it requires a *daily* decision on your part to do a little each day until it just becomes a way of life. Making a few small changes each day will provide you with the peace and confidence you need to move on to mastering bigger things.

One routine that I highly recommend is to be in charge of your mornings, or as Jon Acuff puts it, "Own your mornings." What does this mean? Utilize the morning hours to invest in yourself. Make a decision to be consistent about your own personal development. Highly successful people invest in themselves consistently first thing in the morning. Warren Buffet said, "The best investment you'll ever make is in yourself. It pays a thousand to one."

Why is the morning the best time? For one thing, it sets you up for success the rest of the day. The morning is when you have the most control over your day. It's the time to be most productive. Why? Because people and priorities haven't invaded your attention. It affects your outlook on the rest of the day. You start the day right. Your willpower is at its highest in the morning. The longer the day goes on, the more fatigued we become. So, start the day feeling productive and accomplished.

Get into a habit of spending some alone time in prayer, reading, meditating, journaling, writing your gratitude list or praying over your dreams and goals. Entrepreneur Magazine did research on the habits of the wealthy versus the habits of the poor and discovered that wealthy people wake up three or more hours before they go to work. Why? To invest in themselves. Did you know that waking up just one hour earlier each day would add an extra 15 days to your year? What could you accomplish with an extra 15 days this year? Establishing a morning routine has been pivotal in my life and ministry. It's something I am protective of.

In addition to investing in myself, I began learning from organizing experts how having a routine for your everyday mundane tasks alleviates stress and being overwhelmed all week with tedious chores piling up. For example, establishing a routine for your tasks could include: Pay bills on Sunday night. Do laundry on Saturday mornings. Exercise Monday through Friday. Vacuum on Wednesdays. Call Grandma on Tuesdays. Grocery shopping on Mondays.

When you designate certain days to tackle these tasks, it doesn't stress you out on Wednesday evening when you drive by the mailbox to collect the mail and suddenly think of all the bills you need to pay after you make dinner, give the kids a bath, and visit with your spouse. Why? Because bill paying day is Sunday evening. So, take the mail to the designated spot marked for mail and go about your business.

It's the same with laundry. You won't stress out when you walk into your kid's bathroom Thursday morning and see the pile of dirty towels on the floor. You'll pick them up, toss them in the hamper, and not think about it again until Saturday morning when it's laundry day.

One of the most effective ways to keep your life organized is to make it a part of your routine. Remember, the secret of your future is hidden in your daily routine. You need to find a schedule that works for you and determine to stick to it.

Granted, there are some spaces, like kitchen counters, that require daily decluttering. Set up procedures in your day-today lifestyle that keep you organized. Yes, this will require some discipline on your part, but maintenance each day is much easier than a complete over-haul each month.

It could mean setting new standards for yourself such as:

- Never go to bed with dishes in the sink.
- Never leave the house with beds unmade.
- Always take the daily mail into the home office.
- Always hang your coat after wearing it.
- Always clean the kitchen immediately after dinner.
- Always put away cosmetics and toiletries before going to work.

Reminder: Distractions are the enemies of focus. You must determine to be productive, focused, and achieve what's most important to you. Anyone can improve his or her focus with a little motivation. Planning gives direction to your life. It enables you to live with vision, purpose, and meaning. You set yourself up for success by having a design for each day. You make better decisions based on how it fits in your agenda. You achieve your goals with accuracy and precision. As John Maxwell says, "If you want to change your life, change something you do daily." I recommend having a daily plan.

Day-to-Day Organizing Tips to Simplify Your Life

Grocery shopping. Make a master grocery list on your smart phone of all the usual items you typically purchase on your frequent trip to the market. Once the list is made, you don't have to waste time making out a new list before each trip. It's always there.

Packing for a trip. If you travel a lot, make a packing list on your smart phone of all the common items you need for every trip such as: toiletries, phone charger, vitamins, hair supplies, passport, umbrella, medicines, adapters, etc. Again, you won't have to rack your brain before each trip to make sure you thought of everything. Think of it once and then just refer to the list.

Daily routine. Make a list of everything you need to have ready each day before running out the door to school and/ or work. (Briefcase, lunch, school lunches, vitamins, jackets, backpacks, etc.) Place everything at the back door the night before (except the fresh lunch to be made in the morning). As you are hurrying to leave, simply grab everything at the door.

Sporting events. Again, utilize the Notes feature on your phone and make a list of everything you typically need to have an enjoyable day at the soccer/football/baseball game or whatever sporting event (comfortable chair, sunscreen, sunglasses, hat, music, cooler, water, phone, camera, etc.).

Meals. Plan your meals for the week (as best you can). This step in organization prevents stress during the week of trying to figure out what everyone can eat after a long day at work. Each Sunday, you can make a list of each meal for the week and document it in the Notes section of your phone. Alternate the list every other week to reduce stress and anxiety over what to eat. Having this list will aid in your trip to the market, too. You're prepared. You simply get what you need without spending unnecessary money on unplanned food.

Clothing. Choose your clothes the night before and set them out. This prevents arriving late because you couldn't decide what to wear. Never go to bed without planning the next day—even your wardrobe.

Gym clothes. With a little advanced decision making, you will keep your commitment with yourself to exercise by having your gym clothes laid out the night before. Get up, slip them on, and get out the door.

Refrigerator. Start a habit of cleaning out the refrigerator before you go to the market to bring home more refrigerated food.

Holiday shopping. Make a list of each person you regularly shop for during the holidays. Write the gift purchased and the amount spent next to each person's name. This helps with the accidental repeat purchase next year, as well as budgeting an equal amount on specific relatives and friends. Each year, you already have your list for whom to shop.

Your Car. Start a habit of cleaning all trash out of your car every single time you stop to get gas. You have to wait while the gas is dispensing anyway; you might as well be productive.
Other tips to keeping a clean car:
- Always have a trash receptacle. Any small bag will suffice. Immediately place all garbage into the bag so it doesn't pile up in floors and get stuffed in between seats.
- Empty your car each night. As soon as you arrive home, get everything out of the car. Never leave items visible giving thieves an opportunity to break in.
- Add air fresheners. It gives a car a fresh, tidy smell when you keep a light, clean fragrance in your automobile.

Declutter Your Way To Success

Birthdays. We all know that person who remembers every birthday and sends cards out right on time. The odds are that they don't have the most excellent memory for 35 occasions to celebrate throughout the year. They write it down. Write it on your digital calendar with the command to "repeat yearly." It's always there whether you remember it or not.

Passwords. We all have a dozen systems that require passwords. Remembering them can be a real struggle especially when certain devices ask you to update your password each year. List all your passwords for each account, device, and alarm system in a single place. Always update your list as soon as you update a password. Place the list in a safe, secure place such as a home safe that is locked and out of sight or a secure online location that you can access anytime anywhere when needed.

The kids. They need a checklist too. Write out a list of what they need to do each morning before they leave for school as well as what they need to grab before running out the door. Hang it in a place where they'll refer to each morning.

The babysitter. Make a master list on your computer of everything each potential babysitter needs to know. Once you've thought through every bit of pertinent information, there's no need to go through this process with each caretaker. Do it once. When they arrive, print the ready-made list, and go enjoy your night out.

These lists will aid in saving you time in your busy lifestyle and kickstart your life of productivity. Rather than wondering where the day went and casually wasting hours browsing through social media, you can go to bed each night with the calming assurance that you achieved your most important goals for the day.

Chapter 10

Distinguish Yourself: Making Excellence a Habit

No one gets ahead by striving for mediocrity.
Unknown

God can't use you *publicly* until you've gotten victory *privately.*

That's a statement with powerful impact! What you do behind the scenes has more significance than what you do before a crowd. It is all part of the preparation for where God wants to take you next.

Years ago, when I began this journey of personal growth and development with those five little words, *clean up and clean out*, it set me on a path to success. As my environment improved, my mindset improved. As my home was cleaned, my heart got cleaned. As my surroundings had order, my life had order. And it led to massive promotion. This routine of cleanliness and organization had more to do with what God was preparing me for than simply having stacked sweaters, uniform utensils, and color-coded dresses hanging in my closet. It was all about gearing up for greatness.

It's one thing to set aside a day, a week or a month to completely overhaul and declutter your home, but it's an entirely different discipline to *maintain* that order and organization. It is not easy, by any means. And if you're not careful, you can start to complain, dread or feel sorry for yourself for having to work so hard to keep this new standard when those around you seem to be carefree and could care less. I have fallen into that trap many times until one day the Lord said something to me in my prayer time that I believe, not only woke me up, but shifted my thinking and truly changed the trajectory of my life.

He said, "Don't be *average*, and your *life* won't be average." Emphasis on the understood *you* in this command. *You* don't be average, and your life won't be average. Wow!

Think about how that applies to every area of your life. *You* don't be average, and your career won't be average. *You* don't be average, and your *finances* won't be average. *You* don't be average, and your *marriage* won't be average. *You* don't be average, and your *children* won't be average. *You* don't be average, and your *relationships* won't be average. *You* don't be average, and your *body* won't be average. You get the picture.

That phrase changed my life and consequently, changed my lifestyle. It's anything but average. I say this humbly and with extreme gratitude, but since applying this principle to my life, I don't have an average organization. I don't have average friends. I don't speak at average conferences. I don't own an average home. I don't drive an average car. I don't earn the average salary. I don't live an average life, and I don't serve an average God.

As I put more demands on my life to grow, improve, and increase, my lifestyle grew, improved, and increased.

Distinguish Yourself: Making Excellence a Habit

I want you to think of that statement each morning you make the bed, load the dishwasher, go to the gym, save the money, hang up the clothes, fold the towels, read the book, attend the seminar, vacuum the floor, make the declarations, listen to the podcast, budget the finances, learn the new language, and clean out the car. Don't be average, and your life won't be average. It won't! Pursue excellence, and success will pursue you.

Distinguish Yourself

As you develop an above average life, you will distinguish yourself among others. To distinguish means to recognize or treat someone or something as different, make oneself prominent and worthy of respect through one's behavior or achievements. In other words, to rise above average or stand out, you need to behave in a way contrary to the average person.

We know that, as Christians, we're often required to do things differently than everyone else. In fact, we're specifically instructed not to conform to the ways of the world (Romans 12:2), but I believe God has given us instructions on how to distinguish ourselves for success.

Seth Godin points this out in his bestselling book, *Purple Cow*. He explains, "While driving through France a few years ago, my family and I were enchanted by the hundreds of storybook cows grazing in lovely pastures right next to the road. For dozens of kilometers, we all gazed out the window, marveling at the beauty. Then, within a few minutes, we started ignoring the cows. The new cows were just like the old cows, and what was once amazing was now common. Worse than common: It was boring.

"Cows, after you've seen them for a while, are boring. They

may be well-bred cows, Six Sigma cows, cows lit by a beautiful light, but they are still boring. A Purple Cow, though: Now, that would really stand out. The essence of the Purple Cow—the reason it would shine among a crowd of perfectly competent, even undeniably excellent cows—is that it would be *remarkable*. Something remarkable is worth talking about, worth paying attention to. Boring stuff quickly becomes invisible."[51]

God never meant for you to be ignored, to blend in with the crowd, to be average. So how do you stand out? How do you become remarkable or worth talking about? How do you experience rapid growth, increase and promotion? I believe it's by distinguishing yourself with the following seven habits of excellence.

Habit #1. Lead yourself.

Before you can lead anyone else, you must learn to lead yourself. In fact, years ago John Maxwell was teaching leadership at a seminar and agreed to do a Q & A at the end. A young guy with an MBA stood up and said, "John, I love your leadership principles. I kept thinking, 'Man, I wish I had somebody to lead. I wish I had a team to lead. I wish I had a company or a department. Where should I start?" John said, "Good question. Start with you."

In other words, if you wouldn't follow yourself, why should anyone else follow you? His advice was to start developing excellence and leadership qualities in yourself that you could eventually impart to someone else.

A good exercise is to imagine a teenager saying, "I want to learn to be successful. Can I just shadow you for the next five days to observe your habits?"

What would they see? What would they observe about your

daily life (your routine, your rituals, your habits) that would motivate them to want to be like you? Does that compel you to make a few adjustments?

After I graduated from college, I worked for 11 years as a ghostwriter, which may sound somewhat fascinating; however, everything about me was not. My life, my routine, my habits were anything but remarkable. I was the epitome of the average person. I did not grow myself at all. I slept right up until the last minute to get dressed and run out the door to go to work. I listened to the radio all the way to the office. I arrived just barely on time, never early. I worked all day, listened to the radio on the way home, turned on the TV as soon as I walked in the house, got intrigued in other people's lives until time to go to bed, and then did it again the next day...for more than a decade!

Everything about my life was average. My finances didn't increase. My savings account was still on the to-do list to open one day. My investments were nonexistent. I paid my car note every month, my credit cards every month, and lived paycheck to paycheck. I only exercised if vacation was coming. I never read anything for pleasure except the Dallas Cowboys Cheerleaders manual. And each year of my life looked identical to the year before. My life didn't change, nor did I.

Joyce Meyer says, "God will change your circumstances, but He'll change you first." Now, it makes sense to me why in 2002 when I was falling apart and had no vision for my life, I received that directive to "clean up and clean out." Not long after I began following up with action getting my house and my life in order, the Lord made it clear for me to strive for excellence when He said, "Don't be average, and your life won't be average."

Your life will only grow to the extent that you grow. Your

money will only grow to the extent that you grow. Your ministry will only grow, your career will only grow, your marriage will only grow, your salary will only grow, your influence will only grow to the extent that you grow.

That's when I decided to form a simple routine consisting of five habits I would follow every single day for 21 days in order to "lead myself": (1) pray, (2) read, (3) listen to a motivational message, (4) review my dreams/goals, (5) exercise. You may have heard the stories of how I stuck with these five habits for 21 days and after keeping that commitment, I didn't want to stop. I committed to a full month. After 30 days, I aimed for two solid months. After two months, I went for three. That was in 2002, and I haven't stopped. I had no idea that those five habits were enabling me to distinguish myself.

I never dreamed that this handful of disciplines practiced day-in and day-out would promote me from ghostwriting books to authoring books, from attending conferences to speaking at conferences, from watching television to hosting a TV broadcast...and all the financial increase that has come as a result.

You don't be average, and your life won't be average. You may have seen this quote on Instagram or Pinterest that says, "Obsessed is a word the lazy use to describe the disciplined." Be prepared to be ridiculed and criticized for your new standards of excellence and rituals of discipline. But keep in mind, God hasn't necessarily revealed to those who criticize you what He's revealed to you about preparing for promotion. So, just smile and get back to being excellent.

When you study the lives of those who have succeeded the most in their field, you will notice a common theme: They have routines. They have rituals, and they are disciplined in specific areas of their lives. Everyone from Mick Jagger to Lady GaGa, Tony Robbins, Bill Gates, Richard Branson, Jerry Savelle, Oprah Winfrey, etc.

In fact, many of the most successful high achievers (CEOs, celebrities, pro-athletes, etc.) practice "The Hour of Power" which is a great place to start. It includes 20 minutes of prayer, 20 minutes of reading, and 20 minutes of exercise.

Can you imagine a teenager watching you for a week and saying, "Wow! You are so consistent. You do this every single day?" And you respond with my favorite John Maxwell quote, "Yes, the secret of your future is hidden in your daily routine."

When you start leading yourself with good habits, you will rise above mediocrity, separate yourself from the average, and distinguish yourself for success.

Action Step: Start applying the Hour of Power for 30 days.

Habit #2. Expose yourself to greatness.

Where you are is not where you're supposed to stay. God has more for your life, but you'll stay small if you keep a small mindset.

I heard a story about a man who was out fishing one day and couldn't help but notice another fisherman near him doing something odd. Each time he caught a big fish, he would throw it back in the water. When he caught small fish, he would keep it. This went on all day. The watcher became curious and finally asked, "Why do you throw back all the big fish and keep the small fish?"

He responded, "Oh that's simple. All I have is a 10-inch frying pan." In other words, he was missing out on something bigger and greater for his life because of his limitations.

Before we see increase on the outside, we must see increase

on the inside. You can't do better in your life in an area where you have not been exposed. The Bible says, "I pray the eyes of your heart may be enlightened."[52] Enlightened means to shed light upon, to teach, and to expand in knowledge and wisdom.

For example, if you are the smartest one in your group, you need a new group! If everyone around you thinks you're the coolest, the wisest, the wealthiest, the most successful, then you're in the wrong company. You aren't growing if you're always teaching. You need to be around people who make you feel challenged, awkward, uncomfortable, and uneasy. Those are signs you are being stretched...you're growing!

Get around people who make more money than you, who have a nicer, bigger, more organized home than you. Hang out with people who keep their cars clean and their bodies fit. Go to lunch with people who eat healthier than you and budget their finances wiser than you. Learn from those who are doing more than you. It stretches you to the next level. It prepares you for growth in your own life. Following people who are proving success causes you to rise higher.

Not too long ago, I was coming to the end of the year, and I was feeling a little drained. I had traveled all year all over the world, taped podcasts and broadcasts, wrote another book, recorded new audios, had interviews, appointments, conferences, the list goes on and on. I was exhausted and started to complain.

Right when that self-pity started to come on me, I was invited to a famous minister's birthday party.

As soon as I pulled up to the hotel, I was introduced to Pat Robertson in the lobby. He kissed my cheek and said the sweetest things. When I walked down to the ballroom that evening, I was surrounded by John Hagee, Pat Boone, Creflo Dollar, Andrew Wommack, Jesse Duplantis, Dr. Don Colbert, Kenneth Copeland,

and Jerry Savelle! I was surrounded by greatness.

As I sat there that night watching the guest of honor's life story on video of where he started and what he has achieved, I couldn't help but think, "Come on, Terri. You haven't done squat!" Right then and there, I decided to go on a mission that evening: a mission to listen! I didn't want to talk about my life or ministry, I just wanted to listen and learn from others.

Throughout the evening, my discussions with friends included one lady who is growing organic farms across the globe, hosting a TV show, doing TED talks, writing a new book, and speaking in conferences every single weekend.

Another friend was sharing with me their ideas for their new TV show and how excellent they want it to be. They revealed how major influencers have discovered them on TV and met together for an appointment which led to their spending New Year's Eve with the President of the United States.

Then I began listening to people's schedules and how they not only went to the party that night, but were headed to another conference in the morning, then would be flying home to minister that very night and twice on Sunday while getting ready for their team meetings Monday morning!

Needless to say, I got a real, sweet kick in the pants to shake off the self-pity, complaining, emotional drain, to pick myself up by the bootstraps (or stilettos), and get moving!

What am I saying? When you expose yourself to greatness it causes you to rise higher, put greater demands on yourself, set higher standards for your life, and truly distinguish yourself.

The reason people watch a show like Jerry Springer is because after watching that debacle, you look at your own life and think, "Well, I'm not doing so bad after all. I'm actually doing pretty good." Well, yes, compared to that! But you have a higher standard. God is preparing you for excellence not mediocrity. He has an assignment on your life, and it demands a new normal for you. You're not like everyone else. You're being groomed for greatness!

How do you expose yourself to growth if you can't hang out with people of significance? Read their books. That's how I started and still do to this day. I don't attend famous people's birthday parties every weekend. This single habit has brought more increase and promotion to my life than I can even articulate. And it wasn't something that came natural to me. I used to loathe reading. I had to make myself buy a book, set the timer for 20 minutes, and focus. The more I began to practice this each day, the more I began to crave wisdom and knowledge.

Do you know what you are most likely to find by a wealthy person's nightstand? Books. In fact, it's been discovered that the largest homes of the wealthiest people had something in common that lower income homes do not have: a library. Successful people have successful habits and 88% of the wealthiest people in the world read for 30 minutes or more every day.[53]

T. D. Jakes said, "People who have not been exposed are narrow-minded." Statistics show that lower income/less successful people do read, but 79% read for entertainment (in other words, gossip magazines about other people's lives). On the contrary, 94% of wealthy people read to continually improve their own lives.[54]

John Maxwell's dad paid him and his siblings to read books for 30 minutes each day when they were growing up. They may not have seen the benefit of it as children (other than the extra cash in their pockets), but the outcome of this discipline is undeniable. By the time Maxwell, his brother and his sister graduated high school, they were so far ahead of their peers because they increased in knowledge and wisdom, and it set them on a path for success. By the time his brother graduated college, he was a millionaire. By the time John was 28, he had the 10th largest non-profit in the country. And by the time his sister was 27, she was running a hospital in Dayton, Ohio.

Jim Rohn said, "Success is something you attract by the person you become. If you want more, become more." This goes hand-in-hand with my directive from the Lord, "Don't be average, and your life won't be average." If the average person chooses to watch television, then do the complete opposite and go read for 20 minutes. If the average person sleeps late, do the complete opposite and go spend 20 minutes with the Lord. If the average person is lazy, do the complete opposite and go walk around the block for 20 minutes. You don't be average, and your life won't be average.

Exposing yourself to greatness by reading great books will enlarge your capacity to grow. Brian Tracy wrote, "You are locked in place at your current level of knowledge and skill. You can go no further with what you now know. Your future largely depends on what you learn and practice from this moment forward."[55]

James Allen said, "People are anxious to improve their circumstances but they're not anxious to improve themselves, they, therefore remain bound."

What did you do last year to grow?

How many books did you read?

How many hours did you invest in yourself?

How many seminars or conferences did you attend?

What did you learn?

What were you exposed to?

Set some new goals for yourself to read a certain number of books each year. I determined years ago to read at least 12 books a year (that's one per month). Put yourself in a position to be exposed to greatness. Surround yourself with people who are on a higher level, and you will continue to grow.

Action Step: Choose 12 books to read over the next 12 months.

Habit #3. Demand excellence from yourself.

We have thoroughly covered this concept throughout the book proving that when you have an excellent spirit, you are honoring God. When you demand higher standards from yourself, you are preparing for the next level. Stephen Covey says it this way, "Begin with the end in mind."

Before you can have something, you have to first be something. Success always begins on the inside before it shows up on the outside. Excellence is a state of mind that reveals itself in your everyday life. Start seeing yourself and carrying yourself as the person you desire to be. Marie Kondo, bestselling author of *The Life-Changing Magic of Tidying Up*, wrote, "The space in which we live should be for the person we are becoming now, not for the person we were in the past." You need to see yourself as already being where you want to be and begin acting that way now.

Recently, in my prayer time, the Lord began to instruct me to get *everything* in my life excellent by saying, "It is *vital* to where I want to take you." When I receive a directive in prayer, I take it literally. Not only in getting my house cleaned up and in order, but my finances, my health and fitness, my relationships, my filing cabinet, my schedule, my message preparation, my physical appearance, my clothing, my furniture, everything.

Distinguish Yourself: Making Excellence a Habit

Whatever God has given you, take care of it. A can of paint, a reupholstered couch, a new haircut, and pulling some weeds can make a world of difference.

Dress for where you want to go, not just where you are. T.D. Jakes said, "You can't bring that old look into new dimensions. If God gives you a new opportunity, you need to be dressed for it." Naomi told Ruth, before she could go to Boaz, that she had to change her garments. "Get the garments on now!" (Ruth 3:3). Changing your garments means to prepare for something that hasn't even happened yet! *The New American Standard Bible* says, "Wash yourself therefore, and anoint yourself and put on your *best* clothes."

God blesses people who are prepared. Boaz said to Ruth, "...for all my people in the city know that you are a woman of excellence" (vs. 11). They could tell by her appearance, her demeanor, her personal standards that she was a woman distinguished among others. God always promotes excellence.

I want to encourage you to take your organizing and decluttering efforts to a whole new level in this final chapter by making an "excellence checklist." What I mean by this is after you have applied the decluttering action steps and you feel that each room is in the best condition that suits you, now it's time to make it excellent. Excellent means first class, superior, above average.

This means you take an overview of each room again, but this time you look with the eyes of a potential buyer touring your home. Look for the areas needed to make it absolutely first class. If someone wanted to tour your home with the option to buy it, what would they require you to repair, adjust, fix, replace or remove before purchasing it? If that day comes and you decide to move, you'll have to make those changes anyway, so why not do it now so you and your family can enjoy living in a first-class home?

Excellence in your home could mean: paint over the scuff marks on the wall, remove the extension cord draped across the floor, fix the circuit breaker that went out months ago in the gym (I'm speaking from personal experience), scrub the stain on the carpet, shine the hardwood floors, replace the broken window, repair the doorknob, remove the broken printer, toss the under garments with the elastic stretched out, remove the broken elliptical machine, fix the toilet handle in the guest bedroom, etc.

It could mean a variety of different things for each room. Glance at the room with the perspective of a potential buyer and what they would want repaired. Go through your remaining items (after the decluttering process) to answer whether or not it is excellent. If it doesn't make the cut, toss it. Remove it. You are not the person you used to be. You have a new mindset. You are a person being prepared for a major promotion. God is getting you ready in every area of your life so you can handle the vastness of where He's taking you.

Action Step: Make an "excellence checklist."
- Go through every room in your house and make a list of what needs to be done.
- Start with one room at a time (don't look at any other room).
- Start with the room you spend the most time in.
- Stick with that one room until it's done and then move on.

Habit #4. Focus yourself.

Let me ask you, if you're familiar with my messages and ministry, would you be a little disappointed if you invited a friend to come hear me who had never heard me before, and all I talked about was the rapture, the Eastern gate, the red heifer, hermeneutics, and the jubilee hour? You would be a little confused, wouldn't you? Why? Because you were expecting me to discuss your dreams and goals at some point, right? Why? Because that's my passion, my mandate, my message.

You have no idea how many conferences I'm invited to where the overall theme for that year just happens to be: Dream big! Imagine big! Go for your goals! Go to the next level! Vision! Is that a coincidence?

Do you know what types of gifts I receive more than anything else when I check in my hotel rooms for the events I'm speaking at? Dream journals and plaques about dreaming, Paris-related items, and anything with a cupcake on it, including actual mouthwatering, heavenly cupcakes, piled with buttercream icing straight from the bakery.

Why is that? Apparently, I've become known for those things: Dreams. France. Icing. Marketing is all about having a brand or a unique selling point. Branding or being known for something means you have a unique quality that distinguishes you from others.

Starbucks is known for coffee, although they sell scones and muffins. McDonald's is known for hamburgers, although they sell chicken and salads. Subway is known for sandwiches although they sell cookies. In fact, can you imagine going to Subway and the sandwich artist (yes, that's what they're called) says, "I'm so sorry, but we're out of bread today. Can I get you something else?" No. You go to Subway for sandwiches. Nothing else.

Being known for something means you are not a jack-of-all-trades, master of none. You are a specialist.

As a specialist, you receive respect because you are perceived as the expert. Someone said, "It's better to be world class at a *few* things than mediocre at most things." What are you supposed to be world class at? What are you supposed to be known for? Where are you supposed to be single-minded and focused because it's going to cause you to stand out of the crowd?

James 1:8 says, "A double-minded man is unstable in all his ways" (KJV). How many of his ways? All of them. God wants you stable, focused, clear on your mission and vision for life. Being known for something points you in the right direction.

Let me ask you, if somebody had to think of something that reminded them of you, what would it be? When people hear your name, what do they think of? What do they associate you with? What are you supposed to be known for? If I were to ask your friends to share what comes to mind when they think of you, what would they say? What if I asked your spouse, your child, or your associates and co-workers? You know they would have an answer. What adjectives would they use to describe you, and would you like their responses?

For example, when you think of Emmitt Smith, what do you think of? Football. When you think of Leonardo DiCaprio, what do you think of? Acting. When you think of Celine Dion, what do you think of? Singing.

Become so focused that you distinguish yourself. Myles Munroe said, "Carve out a niche for yourself that they can't ignore you." You were not born to do everything. In fact, when you study the lives of people like Joseph, Moses, Paul, John, Jesus, Abraham, their lives were simple. There is this phrase that describes them: *This one thing I do!* Myles Munroe said, "Get to the point where you know your one thing you do!"

When James Cameron was asked how he managed to produce the two highest grossing movies of all time (*Titanic* and *Avatar*), he said "Focus." Cameron said, "You've got to be super focused like a laser to get anything worthwhile done." He said, "When I did Avatar, I was super focused for four years!"

Larry Page, co-founder of Google, said, "You should focus on one important goal and you need to be single-minded about it." When Tom Monagham, founder of Domino's Pizza, was asked the secret of his success, he said, "A fanatical focus on doing one thing well." Bill Gates said, "If you want to be a great software company, you have to be only a software company."

When you dabble in so many things, you become okay at many things but not great at any one thing. Most of the successful people that you admire are not great at everything. They're great at one thing.

Richard St. John, who has one of the highest viewed TED Talks on YouTube, said for 10 years he was all over the place. He was dabbling in business, music, design, photography, sailing, cooking, running; consequently, he was average at many things but not great at any one thing. Finally, he decided to put all his focus on one thing: photography. His goal was to become an expert in photography. As a result, he became a successful advertising photographer and won many awards including "Best Corporate Video in the World."[56]

Focus pays off. Focus helps you choose: (1) your friends, (2) your library, (3) your time, (4) your energy, (5) your priorities, (6) your money.

After growing up poor in Croatia and then Canada, Robert Herjavec (who can be seen on the television series Shark Tank) began devouring biographies about exceptionally successful people. Herjavec said, "That's when I learned that nobody cares about average. Greatness is what counts. If you want to be successful and make a lot of money, or be famous, or whatever it is that you define as success, do one thing and do it better than everyone else."[57]

Action Step: Narrow your focus. Think about the area God wants you to be world-class in and start developing it.

Habit #5. Encourage yourself.

You will behave on the outside the way you talk to yourself on the inside. Interview any successful person and they'll tell you how important positive self-talk is to your success. The Bible says, "David encouraged himself in the Lord" (1 Samuel 30:6, KJV). If you want to distinguish yourself and prepare for promotion, you have to become your own best cheerleader. In fact, I wrote an entire book called *Pep Talk* on learning the language of success through speaking positive declarations. Some people call them affirmations or confessions. They are statements of faith that dictate where you want your life to go.

The most successful people in the world practice this: Olympians, CEOs, celebrities, professional athletes, ministers, etc. It may look like your dreams will never happen, but don't speak it. It may look like it's going to take years to achieve your goals, but don't speak it. It may appear that nothing is working in your favor, but don't speak it!

If you want to know where your life is headed, listen to the words coming out of your mouth.

We get accustomed to saying negative things like:

"I could never afford something like that."

"That's too expensive for me."

"I'm so sloppy."

"I'm just not disciplined."

"I could never be that organized."

"I can't lose weight no matter what I try."

"I could never make that much money."

"I'd never get that job!"

"I could never live in a house like that!"

Stop all those "I could never" statements from coming out of your mouth. You are limiting yourself by your vocabulary. Your words are keeping you locked into the very circumstances you want out of! Steven Furtick says, "After any phrase in your life, practice saying this statement: 'And that's just the way I want it.'" See how this makes you feel:

"I could never be that organized. And that's just the way I want it."

"I can't lose weight no matter what I try. And that's just the way I want it."

"I could never make that much money. And that's just the way I want it."

"I'm just not disciplined. And that's just the way I want it."

If it's not the way you want it, then don't speak it. Proverbs says, "Death and life are in the power of the tongue."[58] Start speaking life over yourself, your circumstances, your new behaviors. Your life will move in the direction of your what's coming out of your mouth.

This principle requires two action steps: (1) Stop speaking negative words. (2) Start speaking positive words. You must refrain from allowing those negative words, thoughts and statements from coming out of your mouth. You may think it, but don't speak it. In addition to putting a restraint on your mouth, you have to take it a step further and *intentionally* speak positive words over your future.

Scripture says we serve a God "Who gives life to the dead and speaks of *nonexistent things* as if they already exist."[59] That's exactly what you're doing when you choose to make faith-filled declarations from your mouth about where you want your life to go. Declare it. Speak it out. Make a bold confession of faith over you, your finances, your family, your household, your career, your future.

Action Step: Make these declarations over yourself.

I am highly favored of God.

I am accomplishing everything God has placed in my heart.

I have the grace of God to help me get my life organized and in order.

I put actions to my faith.

I am highly proactive.

I am expecting breakthroughs in my life.

I am preparing for greatness.

I am comfortable being uncomfortable.

I boldly step out of my comfort zone to obey God.

I expect blessings to chase me down and overtake me.

I am surrounded by big thinkers, big dreamers, and people of big faith.

I have extraordinary opportunities given to me.

I have preferential treatment because of God's favor.

I am disciplined.

Distinguish Yourself: Making Excellence a Habit

I am highly organized.

I am joyful to be around.

I am fulfilling my destiny.

I embrace every new season God has for me.

My gifts are going before me and bringing me before great men.

I am thriving in life.

I have a sharp mind. I have the mind of Christ.

I am equipped for everything God has for me.

I am rising above every obstacle.

I pray with boldness and confidence.

I trust God with my future.

I know that all things are working together for my good.

I am preparing for the next level.

If you'll change what you're saying, you'll change what you're seeing!

Habit #6. Stretch yourself with goals (Discomfort zone).

If you want to distinguish yourself, become a life-long goal-setter. Do you know that the act of sitting down and making a list of goals you want to accomplish this year gets your blood pressure and your heart rate up? You become alert and excited. You feel good about yourself only when you're working toward achieving something that is important to you.

Darren Hardy, the former publisher of *Success Magazine*, has interviewed the most successful people in the world: Howard Schultz, Oprah Winfrey, Warren Buffet, Jeff Bezos, Bill Gates, Steve Jobs, etc. The two traits he found in each of these high achievers were: (1) They are committed to continual learning. (2) They are committed to continual goal-setting.

Traditional goal-setting or New Year's resolutions look something like this: save money, read more, lose weight, get out of debt, get closer to God, be more organized. In fact, the average person makes the same New Year's goals 10 times without success!

Michael Hyatt, an expert on the art of goal-setting, shared the most common mistakes in setting and achieving goals on one of his podcasts titled, "The Top 10 Mistakes Derailing Your Goals."[60] I thought it was so helpful, I wanted to share a few of them with you to help you avoid these common pitfalls.

You set too many goals. I used to set like 43 goals for the year! One of the top ways people lose focus is by having too many targets to aim at. Your attention is fragmented because it's all over the place not achieving any of them. You've heard the phrase, "Man who chases two rabbits catches neither." Research supports that setting 7-10 goals increases your probability of achieving them.

You don't write your goals down. Ask most people if they feel it is important to write their goals down and they will wholeheartedly agree that it is. The sad thing is, even though everyone feels it is vital, hardly anyone does it. Dr. Gail Matthews, of Dominican University in California, did research on goal-setting and wanted to know what the impact was of writing down your goals on paper as opposed to having goals but keeping them mentally in your head. She discovered that the precise act of writing them down gives you a 42% greater probability of achieving the goal even if you don't do anything else.

You can haphazardly say, "I'd like to save $5,000 this year," but chances are that nothing will happen until you write it down.

You don't make your goals specific. You may have a thought that you would really like to earn more money, but until you make it solid, tangible and concrete, it's doubtful that your finances will increase. I met a lady in Colorado who said she finally got specific about the raise she wanted. Rather than complain about her low salary or simply wish she could earn more money, she wrote down exactly what she desired on a Post-it note and pinned it to her vision board. It simply said, "I receive a $10,000 raise." She approached me at a conference to share how her dreams were manifesting by joyfully saying, "Terri, I got my raise!" I said, "Do you mind me asking how much?" She said, "Of course, it was $10,000. That's what I wrote down."

In most cases, our goals are too broad, vague and general. In my organization, we set goals for everything! Every. Thing. We aren't haphazard about anything. We set specific goals for: phone calls, orders, sales, partners, new connections, website visits, Facebook fans, Twitter followers, invitations to speak, attendees at the conferences. Everything! When the vision is clear, the results will appear.

You don't assign a deadline. Deadlines are motivating. They create a sense of urgency. Many people are afraid to set deadlines because they fear they won't make it. It's okay. You can always move the deadline. If you have a desire to write a book, you need to assign a deadline for each chapter and for the completion of the manuscript. If you have a goal to save money, assign a deadline by asking how much and by when. It motivates you to achieve it in a time frame.

You don't stretch outside your comfort zone. I shared earlier how you need to be uncomfortable. If all your goals are in your comfort zone, it doesn't motivate you. It's not persuasive. It doesn't require you to think differently or to even pray about the achievement of it.

Michael Hyatt recommends you set a goal in the "discomfort zone." This is where your big prayers are answered. This is where you look back and say, "Look what God has done!" But the thing about the "discomfort zone" is that it is uncomfortable, challenging, awkward, sometimes painful and stretching. It simply means that you are going to have to grow to achieve these goals.

You don't make your goals visible. This was discovered as one of the biggest reasons goals are not achieved. They are stashed somewhere in the back of a drawer. They are documented on a flash drive never to be referred to again. They are stuffed in between files that are lost forever. Personally, I have a vision board at home with my personal goals, and we have a giant vision board at the office with all our ministry goals located in the hallway for everyone to see frequently. Each week in our team meetings, we read them out loud one by one so they are ever present before us. Is it a coincidence we keep achieving them? Your life moves toward the dominating images you keep

Distinguish Yourself: Making Excellence a Habit

before your eyes.

I really kicked it up a notch in my personal life in 2012 when I practiced what Brian Tracy teaches on goal-setting.

- Get a notebook. (You can start in the companion workbook.)
- Project forward to December 31st of this year. In your imagination, look back over the year, and ask yourself what would need to happen for you to declare that it has been the most amazing year of your life? Whatever it is, write it down.
- Write your top 10 goals for the year.
- Write the same top 10 goals every day for 30 days without looking at what you wrote the day before. If you can't remember all 10 of them, that's okay. It means they weren't all that important to you. Stay focused on the ones you can remember.
- After 30 days of writing and getting them ingrained in your heart, look at them, pray over them and declare them out loud every day. I recommend making a vision board with pictures to match each of the goals.
- Check them off one-by-one.

Action Step: Follow these goal-setting steps listed above to stretch yourself.

Habit #7. Push yourself! Do more than others are doing.

You may have heard the phrase, "People are rewarded in public for what they practice in private." The ones who make it look effortless are the ones who practice the most when nobody is looking. If you want to distinguish yourself, practice, work hard behind the scenes, put in the extra hours.

Success is not like going to a restaurant where you pay the bill after you've enjoyed the dinner. The success you want requires payment in full, in advance, every single time. We've discussed how vital it is that you prepare behind the scenes by demanding a higher standard from yourself. The truth is that nobody wants to model someone who plays *Candy Crush* for three hours a day, watches soap operas all morning and spends their evenings scrolling through their newsfeed to watch others live their dreams.

Successful people in every field are often said to be blessed with talent or even just lucky. The truth is, most of them work harder than the average person can even imagine. But that's just it, they don't want to be average; therefore, they must do things behind the scenes that distinguish them from everyone else.

Basketball great, Larry Bird would shoot 500 free throw shots every morning before his first class. Actor Jim Carey would sit in front of a mirror contorting his face for hours perfecting his skills. Basketball legend Michael Jordan spent his off seasons taking hundreds of jump shots a day until it was perfect. Former Starbucks CEO Howard Schultz continued to work from home even after putting in 13 hour days. Winston Churchill, one of the 20th century's greatest orators, practiced his speeches compulsively.

Vladimir Horowitz, one of the greatest pianist of all time, supposedly said, "If I don't practice for a day, I know it. If I don't practice for two days, my wife knows it. If I don't practice for three days, the world knows it."

Get this phrase ingrained in your mind: People are rewarded in public for what they practice in private.

I was visiting with a pastor one time who was complaining about how busy she and her husband are and how they barely have any time to prepare for their Sunday morning messages. She simply said, "Most of the time, we just wing it." She admitted that they do pray and spend time with the Lord, but message preparation is on the back burner of priorities and time allotted. Consequently, the church hasn't grown. The funds are scarce. They can barely pay their bills. Each month is a financial struggle. Scripture says to "study to show yourself approved" (2 Timothy 2:15, MEV). We have to put in the extra effort if we want to see the extra rewards.

If you only knew how many hours it takes me to prepare one message, you would be shocked. I really haven't counted the time, but trust me, one 45-minute talk requires hours and hours of research and preparation. Sometimes I feel like something is wrong with me when I see others whip together a sermon, a talk, a presentation in no time, and I'm investing days just gathering information! Then, one day I heard this statement, "The quality of your preparation determines the quality of your performance."

When I go back to the life-changing command the Lord gave me, "Don't be average, and your life won't be average," I am reminded that I don't want to deliver an average message which means I can't settle for an average preparation.

Joel Osteen said, "If you're at the same skill level you were at five years ago, you're at a major disadvantage. Don't get stagnant. Keep working on your skills." Every Sunday after his final service, he sits with a television editor. He studies each broadcast to get it better. He evaluates the lighting, the production, the camera angels, the way he told a story, whether or not he was talking too fast or too slow. He edits out the stumbles and stutters. Joel said, "I don't have to do that, but I want it to be the best it can be." He said, "I don't want to be at this same level next year." Consequently, he pastors the largest church in America.

Actor Will Smith said, "The separation of talent and skill is one of the greatest misunderstood concepts for people who want to excel and have dreams. Talent comes naturally. Skill is only developed by hours and hours and hours of beating on your craft." Smith said, "I've never really viewed myself as particularly talented. Where I excel is with ridiculous, sickening work ethic. While the other guy is sleeping, I'm working. While the other guy is eating, I'm working."

Successful people have the habit of doing what unsuccessful people don't want to do. Excellence not mediocrity. Discipline not disorder. Proactiveness not procrastination. Order not confusion. A routine not a rut. A person prepared for promotion.

God is setting you up for success! Don't feel sorry for yourself. Don't compare yourself to what others are doing or aren't doing. God is calling you to come up higher because His plan for your life requires this preparation. I love what the Lord told Joyce Meyer after she started to wonder why so many high demands for excellence were placed on her life while others could get by with sloppy living, lower standards, and less discipline. The Lord said, "You've asked me for a lot. Do you want it or not?"

It's time to distinguish yourself, set higher standards, move from mediocrity, exit average, and prepare for promotion. As you apply the five simple words of wisdom, clean up and clean out, you won't be average, and your life won't be average.

Whatever you do, work heartily, as for the Lord and not for men.
Colossians 3:23

Notes

1. "How to Make a Military Bed With Hospital Corners." About. com. http://usmilitary.about.com/video/How-to-Make-Military-Corners.htm

2. Texas Exes, "University of Texas at Austin 2014 Commencement Address – Admiral William H. McRaven" YouTube. 2014, May 19, https://www.youtube.com/watch?v=pxBQLFLei70

3. KJV

4. "Surprising Stats." Simply Orderly, http://simplyorderly.com/surprising-statistics/

5. MacVean, Mary, "For Many People Gathering Possessions is Just the Stuff of Life." Los Angeles Times, 2014, March 21, http://articles.latimes.com/2014/mar/21/health/la-he-keeping-stuff-20140322

6. "Surprising Stats." Simply Orderly, NAPO, http://simplyorderly.com/surprising-statistics/

7. "Clean Freaks." Newsweek, 2004, June 6

8. "Surprising Stats." Simply Orderly, NAPO Media Stats, http://simplyorderly.com/surprising-statistics/

9. "Surprising Stats." Simply Orderly, Direct Mail Association, http://simplyorderly.com/surprising-statistics/

10. "Surprising Stats." Simply Orderly, Harris Interactive, http://simplyorderly.com/surprising-statistics/

11. Becker, Joshua. "The Statistics of Clutter." BecomingMinimalist, Jan. 2010, https://www.becomingminimalist.com/the-statistics-of-clutter/

12. Campbell, Louise Firth, and Shapiro, Amram. "The Odds of Actually Keeping Your New Year's Resolution." Huffington Post, 2014, March 17, http://www.huffingtonpost.com/louise-firth-

campbell-/post_6564_b_4602842.html

13. Cronstrom, Kendell. *Real Simple: The Organized Home*. Oxmoor House, 2006. Print.

14. "IKEA US Life at Home Report." http://lifeathome.ikea.com/home/

15. Threlfall, Daniel. "Do These 5 Things at the End of Every Day, and You Will Become More Productive." Huffington Post, 2017, March 10, http://www.huffingtonpost.com/daniel-threlfall/do-these-5-things-at-the-end-of-every-day-and-you-will-become-more-productive_b_9411526.html

16. Von Bergen, Jane M., "So many reasons to neaten up, but it's too imposing." Boston Globe, 2006, March 12, http://archive.boston.com/jobs/news/articles/2006/03/12/so_many_reasons_to_neaten_up_but_its_too_imposing/

17. "Surprising Stats." Simply Orderly, Day Runner Survey, http://simplyorderly.com/surprising-statistics/

18. George, Liana. "How Much Does Disorganization Cost?" By George Organizing Solutions, http://www.bygeorgeorganizing.com/how-much-does-disorganization-cost/

19. Harvey, Julie. "2011 Workplace Organization Survey by OfficeMax" *The SpaceMaster Speaks*, 2011, February 7, https://thespacemaster.wordpress.com/2011/02/07/what-does-your-disorganization-say-about-you/

20. NAPO, "NAPO Public Quick Poll." 2009, January 6, http://www.akorganizing.com/category/time-management/

21. Alban, Deane. "Declutter Your Life for Less Stress, Better Mental Health." Be Brain Fit. https://bebrainfit.com/declutter-stress-health/

22. Rainey, Dennis. "If You Want More, You Must Be Faithful in Little." FamilyLife, http://www.familylife.com/articles/topics/faith/essentials/growing-in-your-faith/if-you-want-more-you-

must-be-faithful-in-little

23. Beck, Melinda. "The Psychology of Clutter," Wall Street Journal, 2014, July 8, https://www.wsj.com/articles/the-psychology-of-clutter-1404772636

24. Harvey, Julie, "What Does Your Disorganization Say About You?" The SpaceMaster Speaks, 2011, February 7, https://thespacemaster.wordpress.com/2011/02/07/what-does-your-disorganization-say-about-you/

25. Tracy, Brian. "Maximum Achievement." Simon Schuster, 1995. Print.

26. Doland, Erin. "Scientists find physical clutter negatively affects your ability to focus, process information." Unclutterer, 2011, March 29, https://unclutterer.com/2011/03/29/scientists-find-physical-clutter-negatively-affects-your-ability-to-focus-process-information/

27. Sholl, Jessie. "The Emotional Toll of Clutter." *Experience Life*, April 2013, https://experiencelife.com/article/the-emotional-toll-of-clutter/

28. Enavati, Amanda. "Why clutter matters and decluttering is difficult." Yahoo! News, 2012, June 25, https://www.yahoo.com/news/blogs/spaces/why-clutter-matters-decluttering-difficult-232127340.html

29. Steel, Piers. *The Procrastination Equation*. Random House Canada, 2010. Print.

30. Miller, Janet. "7 Counterintuitive Tips for Beating Procrastination." Fast Company, 2016, February 24, https://www.fastcompany.com/3057022/7-counterintuitive-tips-for-beating-procrastination

31. Borsheim, Sherry. "Organizing & Time Management Statistics." Simply Productive, 2012, March 12, http://www.simplyproductive.com/2012/03/time-management-statistics/

32. Becker, Joshua. "21 Surprising Statistics That Reveal How Much Stuff We Actually Own." Becoming Minimalist, March 2017, https://www.becomingminimalist.com/clutter-stats/

33. "How to Stop Junk Mail in 6 Easy Steps." Eco-Cycle Inc. 2011, http://www.ecocycle.org/junkmail

34. Trapani, Gina. "Jerry Seinfeld's Productivity Secret." LifeHacker, 2007, July 24, http://lifehacker.com/281626/jerry-seinfelds-productivity-secret

35. Ruhlin, Whitney. "How much each 'Seinfeld' star is worth today." AOL Finance, 2016, May 23, https://www.aol.com/article/2016/05/23/how-much-each-seinfeld-star-is-worth-today/21382177/

36. Scott, Elizabeth. "The Cost of Clutter." VeryWell, 2016, December 12, https://www.verywell.com/the-cost-of-clutter-3144688

37. McMaken, Linda. "The High Cost of Clutter." Investopedia, 2012, September 17, http://www.investopedia.com/financial-edge/0912/the-cost-of-clutter.aspx

38. Ibid.

39. Gillett, Rachel. "6 Most Popular Resolutions Your Coworkers Are Making." Business Insider, 2017, January 2, http://www.businessinsider.com/common-workplace-new-years-resolutions-2016-12

40. McCarthy, Niall. "Survey [Infographic]." Forbes, 2016, September 23, https://www.forbes.com/sites/niallmccarthy/2016/09/23/survey-69-of-americans-have-less-than-1000-in-savings-infographic/#11b4a8b41ae6

41. Miller, Jen A. "Sell Your Junk for Cash." Bankrate, 2010, July 16, http://www.bankrate.com/personal-finance/smart-money/4-ways-to-get-cash-for-your-junk/

42. Faris, Paula. "Turn Unused Clutter Into Cash Just in Time for

the Holidays." ABC News: World News, 2013, November 14, http://abcnews.go.com/blogs/lifestyle/2013/11/turn-unused-clutter-into-cash-just-in-time-for-the-holidays/

43. Washington, Patrice C. "5 Steps to Turn Clutter into Cash This Spring." Real Money Answers, http://realmoneyanswers.com/5-steps-to-turn-clutter-into-cash-this-spring/

44. Faris, Paula. "Turn Unused Clutter Into Cash Just in Time for the Holidays." ABC News: World News, 2013, November 14, http://abcnews.go.com/blogs/lifestyle/2013/11/turn-unused-clutter-into-cash-just-in-time-for-the-holidays/

45. Mayfield, Julie. "Almost Like Printing Cash." The Penny Hoarder, 2014, July 8, https://www.thepennyhoarder.com/jobs-making-money/side-gigs/make-money-from-your-used-ink-cartridges/

46. Harbour, Brian. *Rising Above the Crowd.* Baptist Sunday School Board, 1988. Print.

47. Many of these ideas came from redbookmag.com, OneCrazyHouse.com, hgtv.com.

48. Morgenstern, Julie. *Time Management from the Inside Out.* Holt Paperbacks, 2004. Print.

49. Corley, Tom C. *Rich Habits – The Daily Success Habits of Wealthy Individuals.* Langdon Street Press, 2010. Print.

50. Trapani, Gina. "Work Smart." Fast Company, 2010, March 22, https://www.fastcompany.com/1592454/work-smart-do-your-worst-task-first-or-eat-live-frog-every-morning

51. Godin, Seth. Purple Cow. Portfolio Hardcover, 2003. Print.

52. Ephesians 1:18

53. Corley, Tom C. "16 Rich Habits." Success. 2016, September 8, http://www.success.com/article/16-rich-habits

54. Corley, Tom C. *Rich Habits – The Daily Success Habits of Wealthy Individuals.* Langdon Street Press, 2010. Print.

55. Tracy, Brian. "Maximum Achievement." Simon Schuster, 1995. Print.
56. St. John, Richard. "The 8 Traits Successful People Have in Common," *The Importance of Focus*, TedEd, https://ed.ted.com/lessons/the-importance-of-focus-richard-st-john
57. Shandrow, Kim Lachance. "Robert Herjavec: The World Doesn't Reward Mediocrity." *Entrepreneur*. 2015, July 1, https://www.entrepreneur.com/article/247927
58. Proverbs 18:21, NKJV
59. Romans 4:17, AMP
60. Hyatt, Michael. "The Top 10 Mistakes Derailing Your Goals [Podcast]." *This is Your Life Podcast*, 2016, December 5, https://michaelhyatt.com/podcast-derailing-goals.html

For years, Terri Savelle Foy's life was average. She had no dreams to pursue. Each passing day was just a repeat of the day before. Finally, with a marriage in trouble and her life falling apart, Terri made a change. She began to pursue God like never before, develop a new routine and discovered the power of having a dream and purpose.

As Terri started to recognize her own dreams and goals, she simply wrote them down and reviewed them consistently. This written vision became a road map to drive her life. As a result, those dreams are now a reality.

Terri has become the CEO of an international Christian ministry. She is an author, a conference speaker, and a success coach to hundreds of thousands of people all over the world. Her best-selling books *Make Your Dreams Bigger than Your Memories*, *Imagine Big*, and *Pep Talk* have helped people discover how to overcome the hurts of the past and see the possibilities of a limitless future. Her weekly podcast is a lifeline of hope and inspiration to people around the world.

Terri Savelle Foy is a cheerleader of dreams and is convinced that "if you can dream it, God can do it." She is known across the globe as a world-class motivator of hope and success through her transparent and humorous teaching style. Terri's unique ability to communicate success strategies in a simple and practical way has awakened the dreams of the young and old alike.

Terri shares from personal experience the biblical concepts of using the gift of the imagination to reach full potential in Jesus Christ. From stay-at-home moms to business executives, Terri consistently inspires others to go after their dreams. With step-by-step instruction and the inspiration to follow through, people are fueled with the passion to complete their life assignment down to the last detail (see John 17:4).

Terri and her husband, Rodney Foy, have been married since 1991, and are the parents of a beautiful redheaded daughter, Kassidi Cherie. They live near Dallas, Texas.

Terri Savelle Foy Ministries
Post Office Box 1959
Rockwall, TX 75087
www.terri.com

Other books by Terri Savelle Foy

Make Your Dreams Bigger Than Your Memories

Untangle

Imagine Big

You're Valuable To God

The Leader's Checklist

Dream It. Pin It. Live It.

Pep Talk

CONNECT WITH TERRI

SUBSCRIBE TO THE WEEKLY PODCAST AT

YOUTUBE.COM/TERRISAVELLEFOY

ITUNES

TERRI.COM

Printed in Great Britain
by Amazon